5000 B.C.

and Other Philosophical Fantasies

5000 B.C.
and Other Philosophical Fantasies

Raymond Smullyan

St. Martin's Press
New York

Chapter 5, "Simplicus and the Tree," reprinted with
permission of THE UNIVERSITY of CHICAGO
MAGAZINE, copyright 1975. Chapter 6, "An Epistemological
Nightmare," appeared in *The Mind's I*, edited by Douglas
Hofstadter and Daniel Dennett (New York: Basic Books,
1981).

Design by Kingsley Parker

Library of Congress Cataloging in Publication Data

Smullyan, Raymond M.
  5000 B.C. and other philosophical fantasies.

  1. Philosophy—Miscellanea.   I. Title.   II. Title:
5000 B.C. and other philosophical fantasies.
B68.S65   1983   100   82-17071
ISBN 0-312-29516-2

First Edition

10 9 8 7 6 5 4 3 2 1

Contents

Foreword

When I was in high school, one elderly gentleman, hearing that I was interested in philosophy, said, "You say you are interested in philosophy. Tell me, how would you *define* philosophy?" Before I had time to answer, he continued, "Yesterday, someone from Columbia asked me how I would define philosophy and I told him ...." The gentleman went on talking interminably without ever letting me get a word in edgewise. When he was finished, he said, "Well, it was nice talking to you," and left.

I am quite fascinated by the psychological phenomenon of a person asking a question without the slightest interest in receiving an answer. I am also reminded of Ambrose Bierce's definition of a *bore:* one who talks when you want him to listen. In this particular case, though, it was probably a good thing that the gentleman *didn't* let me answer because I would be sore pressed if I had to give an *informative* definition of philosophy. The literal definition, "love of knowledge," doesn't really give much feeling for what the subject is all about.

The pieces in this volume (at least most of them) are very much what the title suggests—philosophical *fantasies.* Many of them have the flavor of science fiction. There seems to be a new literary form in the air—a form that might aptly be called *philosophical fiction.* I am thinking not only of this book but of such books as *The Mind's I,* not to speak of Hofstadter's earlier work *Gödel, Escher, and Bach.* One advantage of this form, quite aside from the great entertainment value, is that important philosophical issues can be made perfectly comprehensible to the general reader. This book, for example, is completely self-contained. No prior acquaintance with philosophy is presupposed.

Not all the pieces of this volume are fantasies. Chapter 3, for example, is a free-wheeling, light-hearted, rambling collection of miscellaneous observations, anecdotes (some of them autobiographical), jokes, puzzles, and paradoxes. Chapter 4 will be found to contain a historical surprise for many a reader. The fantasies proper are mainly in Parts 3 and 5. Chapter 10 has a special and unusual status.

Although the spirit of this book is almost the opposite of that of a textbook, much of the material has been successfully used in introductory courses in philosophy. Many of the traditional philosophical questions are considered and many different viewpoints are presented—mainly through the various characters of the book. I do not take much of a position myself; I prefer to let my characters argue matters out among themselves. Of course, some of my own biases cannot help but show through on occasions, but I have tried to match opposing characters as evenly as possible.

I am interested in all this as much from a psychological and dramatic perspective as from a philosophical one. Many of the pieces are not so much analyses of philosophical problems as *dramatizations* of philosophical types. As such, I have thought of them largely as theater pieces and I have had great fun presenting them on stage, assisted by various actors and actresses. Audience responses have been most gratifying. I have long believed that the possibilities of successfully using philosophical themes for exciting live dramatic presentations have not yet been fully realized. If this book suggests new possibilities along these lines, then it will have fulfilled one of its principal objectives.

I wish to thank my wife, my friends and colleagues over the years, and Thomas McCormack and Kermit Hummel of St. Martin's Press for their many helpful suggestions.

1

Why Are You Truthful?

1

Why Are You Truthful?

MORALIST: I have gathered you good people together on this occasion because I know that you are among the most truthful people on earth, and so I propose that we hold a symposium on truthfulness. I wish to learn from each of you your reasons for being truthful. Adrian, what is your reason for being truthful?

ADRIAN: My reason is quite simple. It says in the Bible that one should be truthful, and I take the Bible seriously. Since my greatest duty on earth is obedience to the will of God and God commands me to be truthful, my reason for being truthful is obvious.

MORALIST: Very good! And you, Bernard, why are you truthful?

BERNARD: I also take the Bible very seriously. The one thing in the Bible that impresses me most is the Golden Rule: Do unto others as you would have others do unto you. Since I wish others to be truthful with me, I am accordingly truthful with them.

MORALIST: Excellent! And you, Carey, what are your reasons for being truthful?

CAREY: My reasons have nothing to do with religion. I am truthful on purely ethical grounds. I desire to be virtuous, and since truthfulness is one of the virtues and lying is one of the vices, then to be virtuous it is necessary for me to be truthful.

EPISTEMOLOGIST *(who is, strangely enough, in this group though he wasn't invited):* I find this reason peculiar! Carey evidently doesn't value truthfulness in its own right but only because it belongs to the more general category of virtue, and it is this more general category that he values. Indeed, his very way of putting it: "To be virtuous it is necessary for me to be truthful," his very use of the word *necessary* suggests that he is reluctant to be truthful but is nevertheless truthful only as a *means* to another end, that end being virtue itself. This is what I find so strange! Furthermore, I think—

MORALIST: Sorry to interrupt you, old man, but it was not my intention that we criticize the speakers as they go along. I prefer on this occasion to let the speakers simply state their views; we can reserve critical analysis for another time. And so, Daniel, why are you truthful?

DANIEL: My reasons are also nonreligious—or at least nontheistic. I am a great admirer of the ethics of Immanuel Kant. I realize that his ethical attitudes were, at least psychologically, tied up with his religious ones, but many people who reject Kant's theistic views nevertheless accept his moral ones. I am one such person. I am truthful out of obedience to Kant's categorical imperative, which states that one should never perform any act unless one wills that act to be universal law. Since it is obvious that if everybody lied there would be utter chaos, I clearly cannot will it to be universal law that everybody lies. The categorical imperative hence implies that I, too, should not lie.

MORALIST: Very good! And you, Edward, what are your reasons for being truthful?

EDWARD: My reasons are purely humanistic and utilitarian. It is obvious that truthfulness is beneficial to society, and since my main interest in life is to benefit society, then accordingly I am truthful.

MORALIST: Splendid! And you, Frank, why are you truthful?

FRANK: In order to live up to my name. Since my name is Frank, then it behooves me to be frank with people.

MORALIST: Stop being facetious! This is a serious symposium! What about you, George, why are you truthful?

GEORGE: Because I am a selfish bastard!

MORALIST: What!

GEORGE: Exactly! The few times I have lied, I have ended up getting it in the neck! It's not other people I care about; I care about myself. I don't want any trouble! I have simply learned from hard and bitter experience that honesty is the best policy.

MORALIST: What about you, Harry?

HARRY: My ethical orientation is rather similar to that of George. But instead of using the rather harsh phrase *selfish bastard*, I would prefer to classify myself as a hedonist; I perform only those acts calculated to maximize my pleasure in life. I am not as fanatical as George; I place *some* value on other people's happiness but not as much as on my own. And I have much rational evidence that in the long run I will be happiest if I am always truthful.

MORALIST: So you are a hedonist! In other words, you are truthful because it gives you *pleasure* to be truthful, and you avoid lying because you find lying painful. Is that it?

HARRY: Not quite. I do not necessarily derive *immediate* pleasure from being truthful. Indeed, sometimes it is immediately painful. But I am a thoughtful and rational person; I am always willing to sacrifice my immediate pleasures for the sake of my ultimate good. I always plan ahead. Therefore, I am truthful since as I told you I have rational evidence that my being truthful is best for me in the long run.

MORALIST: What is this evidence?

HARRY: That is too long a story for us to go into now. I think we should instead hear the views of the other speakers.

MORALIST: Very good. What about you, Irving?

IRVING: I am also a hedonist.

MORALIST: That so far makes three of you! George, Harry, and you.

IRVING: Yes, but I am not like the others.

MORALIST: How so?

IRVING: You mean how not! By temperament, I feel very different from George, and unlike Harry I am not the rational type of hedonist. Rather, I am a mystical hedonist.

MORALIST: A mystical hedonist? That's a strange combination! I have never heard that one before. What on earth do you mean by a *mystical* hedonist?

IRVING *(sadly):* I don't know!

MORALIST: You don't know? How come you don't know?

IRVING: Well, you see, since I am a mystical hedonist, I am also a hedonist. I feel that if I knew what I meant by a mystical hedonist, I would be less happy than I am not knowing what I mean. Therefore, on hedonistic grounds it is better that I do not know what I mean by a mystical hedonist.

MORALIST: But if you don't even know what you *mean* by a mystical hedonist, how can you possibly know that you are one?

IRVING: Good question! As you say, since I am unable to define a *mystical hedonist,* I couldn't possibly have rational grounds for knowing that I am one. Yet, in fact, I *do* know that I am one. This is precisely where my mysticism comes in.

MORALIST: Oh, my God! This is too complicated for *me!*

IRVING: Me, too.

MORALIST: At any rate, what is your reason for being truthful? The same as Harry's?

IRVING: The reason is the same, but my *justification* of the reason is totally different.

MORALIST: I don't understand. Can you explain this?

IRVING: Why, yes. Like Harry, I believe that my telling the truth is best for me in the long run. But unlike Harry, I have no rational evidence for this. Indeed, all the rational evidence I have is quite to the contrary. Therefore, the *rational* thing for me to do is to lie. But I have a strange intuition that I had best tell the truth. And being a mystic, I trust my intuition more than my reason. Hence, I tell the truth.

MORALIST: Most extraordinary! And what about you, Jacob?

JACOB: My truthfulness is a matter of contingency, not choice.

MORALIST: I don't understand you!

JACOB: I have simply never had the opportunity to lie.

MORALIST: I understand you even less!

JACOB: My attitude is as follows: Obviously, no one in his right mind would ever think of lying to his friends; it only makes sense to lie to one's enemies. If any enemy ever threatened to harm me, I would not for a moment hesitate to lie to divert his attack. But since I have no enemies and never have had any enemies, the opportunity for me to lie has never presented itself.

MORALIST: How singular! And what about you, Kurt; what are your reasons for being truthful?

KURT: I have only one reason. I am truthful simply because I *feel* like being truthful; I have no other reason than that.

MORALIST: But that is no reason!

KURT: Of course it is a reason! As I just told you, it's my *only* reason.

MORALIST: But your reason is no good!

KURT: Whoever said that I had a *good* reason? I said that it's my *reason;* I didn't say it was a *good* one.

MORALIST: Oh, but just because you feel like being truthful, it does not follow that you *should* be truthful. Of course, I believe that you should be truthful but not merely because you *feel* like it. There are many things I feel like doing, but I don't do them because I know that I shouldn't do them. Not everything that one feels like doing is necessarily right! So why is your feeling like being truthful an adequate justification of your being truthful?

EPISTEMOLOGIST: I thought we weren't supposed to argue with the speakers.

MORALIST: I shall ignore that remark. I repeat my question: Just because you feel like being truthful, why does it follow that you should be truthful?

KURT: *Should* be truthful? Who the hell ever said that I *should* be truthful?

MORALIST: Don't tell me now that you believe that you *shouldn't* be truthful!

KURT: Of course not! I don't give a damn what I should or shouldn't do!

MORALIST: Oh, come now; surely you want to do what you believe you ought to do!

KURT: What I *ought* to do! I couldn't care less! Look, man, I don't give one hoot for all your ethics, morality, religion, rights and wrongs, oughts and shoulds! As I told you, I feel like being truthful and that is my only reason.

MORALIST: But I am trying to explain to you that that reason is inadequate!

KURT: I don't give a damm whether it is adequate or not! It so happens I *feel* like being truthful! Do you mind?

MORALIST: No, I don't mind. I don't mind at all. Only you needn't be so belligerent about it! Now what about you, Larry? Why are you truthful?

LARRY: Why does a tree grow?

MORALIST: Look now, we are not here to play mystical games with each other. I asked you a serious question.

LARRY: And I gave you a serious answer.

MORALIST: Oh, come now, what does a tree growing have to do with your being truthful?

LARRY: More perhaps than you realize.

MORALIST: I wish that you would stop giving these cryptic responses! What are you, one of these Zen Buddhists or something?

LARRY: Yes.

MORALIST: Oh, no wonder you talk in this strange manner! But you can't tell me why you are truthful?

LARRY: Can you tell me why a tree grows?

MORALIST: I still don't see what the growth of a tree has to do with your being truthful.

LARRY: More perhaps than you realize.

MORALIST: So we are back to that again! You Zen men are the most frustrating creatures to talk to!

LARRY: In that case, why do you talk to us? But I'm glad you called me a *creature.* That at least shows that you have *some* insight into the true relationship between me and a tree.

MORALIST: Oh, really now, in what significant way are you like a tree?

LARRY: In what significant way am I different?

MORALIST: Oh, surely now, you regard yourself as a *little* more significant than a tree, don't you?

LARRY: Not at all.

MORALIST: But do you not realize that a tree is at a lower stage of life than a man?

LARRY: I find your use of the word *lower* ill advised. It is psychologically misleading and sets an emotional tone that is tantamount to begging the question. I would prefer to say that a tree is at an *earlier* stage of life.

MORALIST: Let's not be pedantic and quibble about words! In this context, *lower* and *earlier* mean exactly the same thing.

LARRY: Oh no they don't! *Objectively* they may have the same meaning in this context but *subjectively* they certainly do not. One would say that a child is at an earlier stage of life than an adult but surely not at a lower stage. This latter mode of speech gives the impression that an adult is superior to a child, which I don't believe many would wish to do.

MORALIST: All right, have it your way; so you're *not* superior to a tree. But why are you truthful? And please don't answer my question again with the question, "Why does a tree grow?"

LARRY: If you tell me why a tree grows, then perhaps I can tell you why I am truthful.

MORALIST: I still don't see the connection between the two! Why must I first tell you why a tree grows?

LARRY: Because I have great difficulty understanding your use of the word *why*. I was hoping that if you told me why a tree grows then I could gather enough data on your use of this word to help me answer your question more satisfactorily.

MORALIST: Oh, so our difficulty is semantical! In that case, I'll use a different word. What is your *reason* for being truthful?

LARRY: Does everything have to have a reason?

MORALIST: Well of course!

LARRY: Really now! Does a tree have a reason for growing?

MORALIST: Of course not. At least, I don't think so.

LARRY: Then why should I have a reason for being truthful?

MORALIST: Because you are not a tree!

LARRY: So because I am not a tree, it follows that I should have a reason for being truthful?

MORALIST: Oh heavens, you are only confusing matters! Look, a tree is not a conscious being; it has no free will and makes no choices. So one would hardly expect a tree to have a reason for growing, but one would expect you to have a reason for what you do!

LARRY: I grant you that if I were not conscious then I would not possibly have a reason for *anything* I do. But it does not therefore follow that because I *am* conscious I must have a reason for *everything* I do. In particular, I have absolutely no reason for being truthful.

MORALIST: No reason? None at all?

LARRY: None whatsoever!

MORALIST: Fantastic! In other words, you are in the same category as Kurt. You feel like being truthful and that is the only reason you are.

LARRY: No, no, not at all! You totally miss my point! As Kurt told you, his feeling like being truthful is, for him, his *reason* for being truthful. But I have *no* reason at all!

MORALIST: You mean that you don't even feel like being truthful?

LARRY: What a strange non sequitur! Of course I feel like being truthful; otherwise I wouldn't be truthful.

MORALIST: So I was right! That *is* your reason for being truthful.

LARRY: I am sorry, but you are still confused. I both feel like being truthful and am truthful but there is no evidence that either of these two phenomena is the reason of the other.

MORALIST: Look, I just can't believe that you have *no reason at all* for being truthful! You *must* have a reason; you just don't know what it is!

LARRY: At this point, I am not sure just which of several possible meanings of the word *reason* you have in mind. When you ask the reason for my being truthful, are you asking for my *motive* or *purpose* in being truthful, or are you seeking the *cause* of my truthfulness? Or are you perhaps asking whether I am truthful out of some *principle* like virtue or duty or obedience to God or the desire to serve humanity or to be personally well off? Which of these meanings do you have in mind?

MORALIST: Take your choice!

LARRY: I would rather you choose.

MORALIST: Very well then. Which of these principles you mentioned is relevant to your case?

LARRY: None of them.

MORALIST: Then what *is* the principle you follow?

LARRY: None whatsoever. I am not truthful on principle.

MORALIST: All right then, let's go over to another of your suggested meanings, cause. What is the cause of your being truthful?

LARRY: I have no idea.

MORALIST: Aren't you helpful!

LARRY: I am trying to be.

MORALIST: You certainly don't *seem* to be trying! At any rate, let's go on to the next possibility. What is your motive or purpose in being truthful?

LARRY: I am not aware of any motive, and I certainly have no purpose in being truthful. Does a tree have any motive or purpose in growing?

MORALIST: Why must you keep picking on that poor tree?

LARRY: Why do you keep picking on *me?*

MORALIST: I'm not picking on you! I'm trying to *help* you. I'm trying to help you to know yourself better.

LARRY: Why on earth should I want to know myself better?

MORALIST: Well, don't you want to?

LARRY: Of course not. Why should I want to do such a foolish thing?

MORALIST: What's so foolish about it? Recall Shakespeare's saying, "Know thyself."

LARRY: I guess it's all right for those who like that sort of thing.

MORALIST: And did not Socrates say that the unexamined life is not worth living?

LARRY: Isn't that a bit on the arrogant side? Who is Socrates to decide which lives are worth living and which not? Does a tree examine its life?

MORALIST: Socrates was talking about human beings, not trees!

LARRY: What is the difference?

MORALIST: Oh, so we're back to that again! Look, I don't have the time to spend with you playing these useless word games! Since you stubbornly deny that your truthfulness is to any purpose, then I think further conversation is futile.

LARRY: Good grief, how you have misunderstood me! I never said that my being truthful is to no purpose!

MORALIST: Of course you did! A short while back you distinctly said that you had no purpose in being truthful.

LARRY: That is true. Indeed, *I* have no purpose in being truthful. But that does not mean that there *is* no purpose in my being truthful. Of course there is a purpose—I feel a very important one —but this purpose is not mine.

MORALIST: Now I don't understand you at all!

LARRY: Isn't that amazing; you understand the matter perfectly with a tree but not with a human! That so beautifully reveals how differently you think of the two. You grant that a tree has no reason or purpose in growing since you say that a tree is not a conscious entity. Yet that does not mean that the growing of a tree *serves* no purpose. Now you will say that since I, unlike a tree, am a conscious entity, I not only *serve* purposes but have my *own* purposes, and indeed I often do. When I came here tonight, I had the definite purpose of speaking with you all. But that does not mean that everything I do I necessarily do for a purpose. In particular, my being truthful serves absolutely no purpose of *mine.* But I do not doubt that it serves a very important purpose. You see now why I compare my being truthful to the growing of a tree?

MORALIST: Yes, now for the first time I begin to get an inkling of what you are saying. I don't think I would agree with your point of view, but I do find it of interest, and I wish we had more time to go into details, but the evening is getting well on, and we should not neglect our final speaker, Simplicus. Actually, I planned this occasion primarily in Simplicus's honor as a tribute to a great and truthful man, one who is probably more truthful than all of us. All of us here tell nothing but the truth, but Simplicus also always tells the *whole* truth. Therefore, he should be most competent to analyze the real purpose of truthfulness. And so we ask you, Simplicus, what is *your* reason for being truthful?

SIMPLICUS: Me? Truthful? I had no idea that I was.

2

A Puzzle

Before leaving the subject of truth telling, I would like to tell you one of my favorite logic puzzles.

Suppose there are two identical twin brothers, one who always lies and the other who always tells the truth. Now, the truth teller is also totally accurate in all his beliefs; all true propositions he believes to be true and all false propositions he believes to be false. The lying brother is totally inaccurate in his beliefs; all true propositions he believes to be false, and all false propositions he believes to be true. The interesting thing is that each brother will give the same answer to the same question. For example, suppose you ask whether two plus two equals four. The accurate truth teller knows that it is and will truthfully answer *yes*. The inaccurate liar will believe that two plus two does not equal four (since he is inaccurate) and will then lie and say that it does; he will also answer *yes*.

The situation is reminiscent of an incident I read about in a textbook on abnormal psychology: The doctors in a mental institution were thinking of releasing a certain schizophrenic patient. They decided to give him a test under a lie detector. One of the questions they asked him was, "Are you Napoleon?" He replied, "No." The machine showed that he was lying!

Getting back to the twin brothers, two logicians were having an argument about the following question: Suppose one were to meet one of the two brothers alone. Would it be possible by asking him any number of yes-no questions to find out which one he is? One logician said, "No, it would not be possible because whatever answers you got to your questions, the other brother would have given the same answers." The second logician claimed that it was possible to find out. The second logician was right, and the puzzle has two parts: (1) How many questions are necessary?; and (2) more interesting yet, What was wrong with the first logician's argument? (Readers who enjoy doing logic puzzles might wish to try solving this one on their own before reading further.)

To determine which brother you are addressing, one question is enough; just ask him if he is the accurate truth teller. If he is, he will know that he is (since he is accurate) and truthfully will answer *yes.* If he is the inaccurate liar, he will believe that he is the accurate truth teller (since he is inaccurate in his beliefs), but then he will lie and say *no.* So the accurate truth teller will answer *yes* and the inaccurate liar *no* to this question.

Now what was wrong with the first logician's argument; don't the two brothers give the same answer to the same question? They do, but the whole point is that if I ask one person, "Are *you* the accurate truth teller?" and then ask another, "Are *you* the accurate truth teller?" I am really asking two different questions since the identical word *you* has a different reference in each case.

2

On Things in General

3

Miscellaneous Fragments

1

Self-annihilating Sentences. Over a period of many years, the computer scientist Dr. Saul Gorn has compiled a delightful collection of sentences that somehow manage to defeat themselves. He has titled this collection "S. Gorn's Compendium of Rarely Used Cliches." With his kind permission, I reproduce a few choice items (with one or two minor modifications).

1. Before I begin speaking, there is something I would like to say.
2. I am a firm believer in optimism because without optimism, what else is there?
3. Half the lies they tell about me are true.
4. Every Tom, Dick, and Harry is called *John.*
5. Having lost sight of our goal, we must redouble our efforts!
6. I'll see to it that your project deserves to be funded.

7. I've given you an unlimited budget, and you have already exceeded it!
8. A preposition must never be used to end a sentence with.
9. This species has always been extinct.
10. Authorized parking forbidden!
11. If you're not prejudiced, you just don't understand!
12. Inflation is an economic device whereby each person earns more than the next.
13. Superstition brings bad luck.
14. That's a real step forward into the unknown.
15. You've outdone yourself as usual.
16. Every once in a while it never stops raining.
17. Monism is the theory that anything less than everything is nothing.
18. A formalist is one who cannot understand a theory unless it is meaningless.

2

Saul Gorn once told me his theory of asceticism: "It is well known that the longer one postpones a pleasure, the greater the pleasure is when one finally gets it. Therefore, if one postpones it forever, the pleasure should be infinite."

3

Many years ago, Saul Gorn and I were having supper at the Automat. Just as Saul finished, a waiter snatched away his plate. "Ah!" exclaimed Saul. "I finished just in time!"

4

On another occasion, Saul and I were with a group of friends. Saul asked us whether we wanted to go to a certain place. We finally decided not to go. Saul looked at us and said, "Then how do you expect to get there?"

5

Saul once told me that he was teaching a class in which two students were always talking to each other. Finally, Saul said, "It's pointless for you to keep talking because if you do, I'll have to talk louder, and then neither of you will be able to hear what the other one is saying."

6

This reminds me of an incident that occurred when I was giving an examination to an undergraduate class. At the beginning of the exam, I said to the class, "Will you give me your word of honor that you won't cheat if I give you mine that I won't report you in case you do?"

7

I am a firm believer that in studying mathematics one should never forget one's common sense. Many years ago, I was teaching an elementary algebra course. On one exam, I had a standard-type question that involved finding the ages of a mother, father, and child. After the students read the question, I said, "On this problem, I'll give you one hint." All eyes eagerly turned to me. I continued, "If the child should turn out to be older than either of the parents, then you've done something wrong."

8

On another occasion, I had to present the Pythagorean Theorem to a class in geometry. I drew a right triangle on the board with squares on the hypotenuse and legs and said, "Obviously, the square on the hypotenuse has a larger area than either of the other two squares. Now suppose these three squares were made of beaten gold, and you were offered either the one large square or the two small squares. Which would you choose?"

Interestingly enough, about half the class opted for the one large square and half for the two small ones. A lively argument began. Both groups were equally amazed when told that it would make no difference.

9

At one university where I taught, we were thinking of hiring a certain candidate. We invited him up for a talk. Sometime after the talk, the chairman asked him how he liked teaching. He replied, "I've never done any, but I don't think I'd like it."

At a departmental meeting a few days later, we were discussing why the candidate said that. "Oh," suggested one of the department members, "he probably dislikes lying even more than teaching!"

10

A Question of Semantics. At a seminar that he was giving, the late philosopher Alan Ross Anderson told the following fascinating incident: Anderson was working for the navy during World War II with a group deciphering Japanese code. They had great difficulty deciphering one word (represented by a number) that kept coming in repeatedly. It was soon apparent that the word was an adjective applying to people and nations ("This nation is————, but that nation is not————."). After much data were received, they finally decoded it as *pro-Japanese.* At the end of the war, the code book was captured, and the true meaning of the word was *sincere.*

11

The philosopher Nual Belnap, Jr., who collaborated with Alan Ross Anderson on a fundamental work in the field known as *relevance logic,* recently introduced me at a talk at Carnegie-Mellon University. He said, "In this introduction, I promised myself three things: First, to be brief. Second, not to be facetious. Third, not to refer to this introduction."

12

Someone once told me that he believed that logicians reason more accurately than other people; they make fewer mistakes.

"Logicians do *not* make fewer mistakes," I replied quite emphatically, "and if I'm wrong about that, then here am I, a logician, who has just made a mistake."

13

Recently, someone asked me if I believed in astrology. He seemed somewhat puzzled when I explained that the reason that I don't is that I'm a Gemini.

14

Because I have been a magician for many years, people have often asked me whether I ever have sawn a woman in half. I reply, "Oh, yes; I've sawn over seventy women in half in my lifetime, and I'm learning the second half of the trick now."

15

I performed magic most intensively when I was a student at the University of Chicago. I never did much stage magic; I was a close-up magician who entertained small groups at private parties and more often at the tables of various supper clubs. The following recollection is about my funniest.

At one table where I was performing, there was a man who was about the most blasé character I have ever met. He just sat there smoking his pipe, saying not a word, and *nothing* I could do got the slightest rise out of him. I made my tricks more and more startling, all to no avail. After about twenty-five minutes of increasing effort, I finally did my most spectacular effect, at which he took his pipe out of his mouth, slammed the table with his fist, and angrily shouted, "It's a *trick!*"

16

In those days, I particularly delighted in playing tricks on the philosopher Rudolf Carnap; he was the perfect audience! (Most scientists and mathematicians are; they are so honest themselves that they have great difficulty in seeing through the deceptions of others.) After one particular trick, Carnap said, "Nohhhh! I didn't think that could happen in *any* possible world, let alone *this* one!"

17

In item #249 of my book of logic puzzles titled *What Is the Name of This Book?*, I describe an infallible method of proving anything whatsoever.[1] Only a magician is capable of employing the method, however. I once used it on Rudolf Carnap to prove the existence of God.

"Here you see a red card," I said to Professor Carnap as I removed a card from the deck. "I place it face down in your palm. Now, you know that a false proposition implies *any* proposition. Therefore, if this card were black, then God would exist. Do you agree?"

"Oh, certainly," replied Carnap, "*if* the card were black, then God would exist."

"Very good," I said as I turned over the card. "As you see, the card *is* black. Therefore, God exists!"

"Ah, yes!" replied Carnap in a philosophical tone. "Proof by legerdemain! Same as the theologians use!"

18

Speaking of proofs of the existence of God, the funniest one I have ever seen was in a term paper handed in by a freshman. She wrote, "God must exist because he wouldn't be so mean as to make me believe he exists if he really doesn't!" Is this argument really so much worse than the ontological proofs of the existence of God provided by Anselm and Descartes, among others? (See Chapter 10.)

19

It has always puzzled me that so many religious people have taken it for granted that God favors those who believe in him. Isn't it possible that the actual God is a scientific God who has little patience with beliefs founded on faith rather than evidence?

20

This reflection on the nature of God may not be too unrelated to the problems raised by Pascal's wager. Pascal says that it is better to believe in God than not to believe because if God doesn't exist and one believes that he does, the loss is trivial compared with the infinite loss incurred if God does exist and one believes that he doesn't. (Failing to believe in a God who exists means eternal damnation, and such a loss is indeed infinite!) Therefore (reasons Pascal), from the objective viewpoint of pure probability, the rational thing to do is to believe in God.

Now, if it were really true that believing in God increases the probability of salvation one iota, then I would agree that one had best believe in God. But why should this assumption be true? I tend to feel that any God who could be so hideous as to damn a soul eternally couldn't be trusted on any issue whatsoever!

21

A delightful counterexample to the attitude described in §19 is that of a Protestant minister I once knew who said to me, "Why is it that the best people I know are atheists?"

"How do you ever expect to convert them *that* way?" I asked.

"Convert them?" he replied. "Who wants to convert them?"

22

When I was quite young I was present during a rather curious conversation. One person said, "I know there is a God!"

Another said, "And I know there isn't."

Isn't it remarkable that two contradictory propositions can both be known? In fact, how can either of these two propositions be known? If there really is a God, could that fact be not merely believed but actually known? Perhaps it could—by, say, some mystical insight. On the other hand, if there isn't a God, could that fact be known? Certainly not by any scientific means! Could it then be known by some mystical means? If so, it would be a rather fascinating type of mysticism that could perceive the nonexistence rather than the existence of something!

23

Curiously, people often confuse the following questions: (1) Is there a God?; and (2) is there an afterlife? Just because many religions believe in both is no reason to assume that the answers are necessarily the same! It could be that there is a God and no afterlife or that there is an afterlife and no God; or it could be that neither exist, or maybe both.

Recently, however, the two questions have become more separated. Indeed, people nowadays tend to be more skeptical about an afterlife than about the existence of God. I wonder why this is?

24

In *The Future of an Illusion,* Freud spends all his time discussing the desirability of civilization's maintaining or rejecting the "illusion" of religion.[2] He tries to project the probable psychological results of outgrowing the illusion, which he feels will be helpful, and he spends much time trying to dispel counterarguments.

To a realistic Platonist like myself, the real question is not whether religion is helpful or harmful but whether it is true. This question Freud hardly considers. He simply takes it for granted that religion is false, and he offers a purely naturalistic explanation of why people believe in God. Now, I have little doubt that even if there is no God people would still believe in one, quite possibly for the very reasons Freud gave. But this sheds absolutely no light on the more fundamental question of the truth or falsity of theism. As others have pointed out so well, a purely psychological explanation of the origins of a belief does not constitute the slightest rational evidence for or against the belief itself. (I wish more Marxists would realize this!)

I think that most parental decisions about giving children religious training, though often rationalized in terms of what is good for the children, are really governed by whether the parents themselves believe in God or not. However, this is not always the case. I knew a father who said, "I myself don't believe in God, but I still think that every child should have religious training." I have wondered why he had this attitude. Did he believe in deliberately lying to a child for its own good? Or did he perhaps believe deep down in God after all but was unaware of the fact?

On the other hand, I have never known anyone who believed in God but nevertheless felt that religious training is bad for a child. And so there is a curious asymmetry between theism and atheism. Though many atheists feel that the belief in God is bad, this badness is not a logical consequence of the doctrine of atheism, whereas in many if not most of the existing religions, the badness of disbelief (as well as the goodness of belief) is implied by the religion itself— indeed, is often explicitly part of the doctrine.

Freud seemed to have been deeply concerned about the general influence his book would have. The book is certainly an interesting one in its own right, but it is doubtful that it ever had or will have much influence at all, especially in either dispelling or cementing religious ties. Religious trends seem to come and go by laws of their own that we do not understand too well, and our choice in these matters is probably less significant than would appear.

25

A solipsist is one who says, "I am the only one who exists." (I am not sure that he actually has to say it; it is probably sufficient that he *believe* it!) At another seminar given by Alan Ross Anderson, about two hours were spent discussing solipsism. At the end of the period, I got up and said, "At this point, I think I've become an *antisolipsist;* I believe that everyone exists except me!"

26

The logician Melvin Fitting, with his typical sense of humor, once said to me, "Of course I believe that solipsism is the correct philosophy, but that's only one man's opinion."

27

This comment is reminiscent of the famous story about the lady who wrote to Bertrand Russell, "Why are you surprised to hear that I'm a solipsist? Isn't everybody?"

28

I have met some actual solipsists. One once said to me, "Smullyan, you don't exist!"

"Just *who* is it that you claim doesn't exist?" I replied.

29

Another solipsist once said to me, "I am the only one who exists."

"That's right," I replied. "I am the only one who exists."

"No, no!" he said. "I'm saying: *I* am the only one who exists."

"That's what I am saying; *I* am the only one who exists."

"No, no, no!" he excitedly shouted. "It is *I*, not *you*, who exists!"

"That's right." I repeated. "It is *I*, not *you*, who exists. We seem to agree perfectly!"

At this point, he became somewhat confused.

30

This exchange brings to mind the definition of *I* given by Ambrose Bierce in *The Devil's Dictionary.* [3] After defining the term, he continues, "Its plural is said to be *we*, but how there can be more than one myself is doubtless clearer to the grammarians than it is to the author of this incomparable dictionary." Despite the levity, the issue Bierce raises is a profound one that we will deal with more fully in Chapter 12, titled "Enlightened Solipsism."

31

I have sometimes wondered how a militant solipsist would react if everybody, instead of arguing with him, simply agreed with him! I once asked a professional psychiatrist what he thought. He replied, "I imagine that he would be terrified!"

32

Speaking of psychiatrists, I once heard the following anecdote about Freud. Someone asked him, "Would you hold a man responsible for what he dreams?" Freud replied, "Whom else would you hold responsible?"

33

The following exchange once occurred between a disciple of Freud and one of his patients.

PATIENT: Doctor, if you help me, I'll give you every penny I possess!

PSYCHIATRIST: I shall be satisfied with thirty kronen an hour.

PATIENT: But isn't that rather excessive?

34

Turning from psychiatrists to philosophers, a philosopher once had the following dream: First Aristotle appeared, and the philosopher said to him, "Could you give me a fifteen-minute capsule sketch of your entire philosophy?" To the philosopher's surprise, Aristotle gave him an excellent exposition in which he compressed an enormous amount of material into a mere fifteen minutes. But then the philosopher raised a certain objection that Aristotle couldn't answer. Confounded, Aristotle disappeared. Then Plato appeared. The same thing happened again, and the philosopher's objection to Plato was the very same as his objection to Aristotle. Plato also couldn't answer it and disappeared. Then all the famous philosophers of history appeared one by one, and our philosopher refuted every one with the same objection. After the last philosopher vanished, our philosopher said to himself, "I know I'm asleep and dreaming all this. Yet I've found a universal refutation for all philosophical systems! Tomorrow when I wake up, I will probably have forgotten it, and the world will really miss something!" With an iron effort, the philosopher forced himself to wake up, rush over to his desk, and write down his universal refutation. Then he jumped back into bed with a sigh of relief. The next morning when he awoke, he went over to the desk to see what he had written. It was, "That's what *you* say!"

35

There is a story about a philosopher who went into a closet for ten years to contemplate the question, What is life? When he came out, he went into the street and met an old colleague, who asked him where in heaven's name he had been all those years.

"In a closet," he replied. "I wanted to know what life really *is.*"

"And have you found an answer?"

"Yes," he replied. "I think it can best be expressed by saying that life is like a bridge."

"That's all well and good," replied the colleague, "but can you be a little more explicit? Can you tell me *how* life is like a bridge?"

"Oh," replied the philosopher after some thought, "maybe you're right; perhaps life is not like a bridge."

36

There is also a story about Epimenides, who once became interested in Eastern philosophy and made a long pilgrimage to meet

Buddha. When he finally met him, Epimenides said, "I have come to ask a question. What is the best question that can be asked and what is the best answer that can be given?"

Buddha replied, "The best question that can be asked is the question you have just asked, and the best answer that can be given is the answer I am giving."

37

Cartesian philosophy is the philosophy of René Descartes. Descartes first set out to prove his own existence. His proof is remarkably short; it consists of only three Latin words: "Cogito, ergo sum," that is, "I think, therefore I am." When I first heard this, I couldn't resist writing the following verse:

> I think, therefore I am?
> Could be!
> Or is it really someone else who only thinks he's me?

Descartes was a dualist; he believed that mind and matter are separate substances. Idealists like George Berkeley believe that nothing exists but mind. (The *absolute* idealist furthermore believes that there is only one mind in the universe.) At the opposite pole are the materialists (or realists, as they are sometimes called) who believe that nothing exists but matter and energy.

I have asked many children, "Do you believe that your mind is the same thing as your brain?" Interestingly enough, about half answered *yes* and half answered *no*. Among those who answered *no*, one said, "The mind cannot be the same thing as the brain because the brain is something tangible and the mind is not."

38

By now, I have defined just about all the technical terms that will be used in this book. I should add that epistemology is the theory of knowledge and should also say a word or two about logical positivism.

If I were to write a devil's philosophical dictionary in the style of Ambrose Bierce, I would define a logical positivist as one who rejects as meaningless any statement that he is incapable of understanding. Prejudicial as this definition certainly is, it is not completely without truth. Actually, the logical positivists set up (presumably) precise criteria of meaning, and any statement not passing these criteria is declared meaningless. But it can be argued that in setting up their criteria, they take into account only those meanings that they can understand.

Let me tell you a relevant true story: I once dined at a country inn. To my surprise, the walls of the dining room were lined with bookshelves that held a magnificent philosophical library.

"Oh, yes," the proprietress later explained, "my ex-husband is a philosopher and left me this library. He is a logical positivist, and it was logical positivism that broke up our marriage."

"Now, how could that be?" I exclaimed.

"Because everything I said—whatever it was—he kept telling me was meaningless!"

39

One of the basic principles of logical positivism is that no sentence should be regarded as meaningful unless there is, in principle, some method of verifying whether it is true or false. Of course, many people are logical positivists in this sense even though they have never heard the term *logical positivism.*

On the nicer side of logical positivism, I believe the pianist Artur Schnabel must have been one such person. I once attended three fascinating lectures given by Schnabel at the University of Chicago. During one of the question periods, someone asked him what he thought of his latest review.

"I don't read my reviews," replied Schnabel, "at least not in America. The trouble with American reviewers is that when they make a criticism, I don't know what to do about it! Now, in Europe it was different—for example, I once gave a concert in Berlin. The critic wrote, 'Schnabel played the first movement of the Brahms sonata too fast.' I thought about the matter and realized that the man was right! But I knew what to do about it; I now simply play the movement a little slower. But when these American critics say things like, 'The trouble with Schnabel is that he doesn't put enough *moonshine* in his playing,' then I simply don't know what to do about it!"

40

At another lecture, Schnabel said, "You may find this hard to believe, but Igor Stravinsky has actually published in the papers the statement, 'Music to be great must be completely cold and unemotional'! And last Sunday, I was having breakfast with Arnold Shönberg, and I said to him, 'Can you imagine that Stravinsky actually made the statement that music to be great must be cold and unemotional?' At this, Schönberg got furious and said, 'I said that first!' "

41

Sometime around 1940, the composer Leon Kirchner, then a student, was visiting me in New York. We listened to Schnabel's recording of Schubert's posthumous Sonata in A and were both deeply moved. (This is as good a piano recording as has ever been made!)

"Why don't we phone up Schnabel and congratulate him?" I jokingly suggested.

Leon immediately rushed to the phone. I went into another room and with great trepidation listened in on an extension. Schnabel was in and Leon told him how he and a friend had just listened to the recording and were so impressed by his remarkable understanding of the architecture of the piece that we *had* to phone him and let him know. Naturally, Leon and I were both extremely nervous at the idea of taking up the time of the great Schnabel. But what happened was this:

"Ah, yes," said Schnabel, "now you see, the first movement of the sonata is still a classic movement, whereas the second movement . . . " Schnabel went on and on, keeping *us* on the phone for about an hour as he traced the entire development of the sonata form!

42

On one occasion when I visited Schnabel, he was in a rather philosophic mood. "Oh, yes," he said, "I am a realist! It is because I am a realist that I can sit back and be an idealist!" Seeing my look of bewilderment, he added, "Because *ideals* are the reality!"

43

The composer Paul Hindemith was once conducting a rehearsal of one of his more dissonant orchestral compositions. At one point, he rapped his baton and said, "No, no, gentlemen; even though it sounds wrong, it's still not right!"

44

The pianist Leopold Godowsky once visited a composer-friend and found him composing merrily away with operatic scores all over the piano. Godowsky said, "Oh, I thought you composed from memory!"

45

I once heard a radio interview with the pianist Artur Rubinstein. On the whole, the interviewer struck me as incredibly trite and stupid. Out of the blue, he asked, "Mr. Rubinstein, do you believe in God?" There was a tense pause. "No," replied Rubinstein, quite definitely. "You see, what I believe in is something much greater!"

46

This anecdote reminds me of a riddle: What is it that's greater than God; the dead eat it, and if the living eat it, they die? (See §53, for answer.)

47

When Mark Twain was asked what he thought of the music of Richard Wagner, he replied, "Oh, it's probably not as bad as it sounds!"

48

Music and Mathematics. The mathematician Felix Klein was once at a party where the company was discussing the correlation between mathematics and music with respect to both tastes and aptitudes. Klein looked more and more puzzled and finally said, "But I don't understand; mathematics is beautiful!"

49

Pitch and Color. Our visual spectrum happens to be less than one octave, that is, the highest frequency of light that we humans can perceive is not quite twice the lowest frequency. (By contrast, our auditory spectrum encompasses several octaves.) If our visual spectrum were a little more than an octave, I wonder whether two colors an octave apart would have the same psychological similarity as two notes an octave apart.

I once put this question to a rather famous Italian physiologist. He replied, "Ah, that's a beautiful question!" I also put it to an equally famous musicologist. He answered in an irritated tone, "That's obviously unverifiable!" So you see, the musicologist was really a logical positivist at heart (in the bad sense), whereas the physiologist was not.

But is the question really unverifiable *in principle?* Is it inconceivable that science might one day find a means of extending our visual spectrum? Perhaps it is. But isn't it possible that we might one day meet intelligent beings from another planet whose visual spectrum *is* more than an octave and simply ask them?

50

Absolute Pitch. I was once riding in the front seat of a car driven by the computer scientist Dr. Marvin Minsky. In the backseat were two scientists from Bell Telephone Laboratories. The conversation turned to the subject of absolute pitch. Marvin said to them, "You know, Ray here has absolute pitch." One of the two asked me, "How accurate is your sense of absolute pitch?" For some odd reason or other, I didn't hear the question, so he said somewhat louder, "I say, how accurate is your sense of absolute pitch?" Upon which, Marvin turned around and said to them, "Oh, I forgot to tell you—he's also deaf!"

51

Once at a mathematics conference, one of the speakers gave me an account of a paper he was about to deliver. I found the account incomprehensible. As he was talking, Marvin Minsky walked by and said to him, "No, no; your trouble is that you're confusing a thing with itself!"

52

I love Marvin Minsky's quote on the jacket cover of the book *The Mind's I.* [4]

This great collection of reflections provides you with your own quite special ways to understand things such as why, if you don't read this book, you'll never be the same again.

53

The answer to the riddle of §46 is *nothing*.

54

I have told several philosophers that despite my great love for the Taoist philosophers Laotse, Chuangtse, and Liehtse, perhaps my favorite philosopher of all is Ferdinand the Bull. One of them took this seriously and earnestly tried to convince me that Ferdinand couldn't be a philosopher. "A philosopher is necessarily human," he said. I can't see why this must be true! Didn't Ferdinand have a pacifist philosophy?

55

I read in some philosophy book or other that perhaps the one true philosopher was the little girl of nine who was looking out a window and suddenly turned to her mother and said, "But what puzzles me is why there is anything at all!" The following comments, made by children I have known, have definite philosophical overtones.

Vincent (aged 3). When Vincent was about to go up in an airplane for the first time, he asked his father, "When we go up, will we also get small?"

Barry (aged 5 or 6). Barry once said, "I hope I never get to be ninety-nine!"

"Why?" I asked.

"Because when you get that old, you could die!"

Miriam (aged 8). Miriam is the daughter of a mathematical logician. She has either inherited or acquired many of her father's characteristics. At one point during dinner, her father said, "That's no way to eat, Miriam!"

She replied, "I'm not eating Miriam."

Jennifer (aged 6). Jennifer is the daughter of a philosopher. One morning, her brother Jon (aged 8) came down to breakfast and played one April Fools' joke after another on the parents. Then Jennifer came down, and Jonny tried an April Fools' joke on her.

"What's the matter with you, Jonny," she said. "Today's not April Fool!"

"It isn't?" he cried in astonishment.

"April Fool!"

On another occasion, Jennifer had just come home from a movie. She said to her mother, "Mommy, what is the best movie ever made? And I don't want you to tell me what you *think* is the best movie; I want you to tell me what *is* the best movie."

David (aged 10). My wife and I were once with David's family at a drive-in theater. The first feature was excellent, but the second feature looked as if it were going to be terrible. One of the adults suggested that we leave. David of course wanted to stay, and so an argument began.

"Why don't we take a vote?" I suggested.

"No!" said David. "That's not fair because the majority will win!"

Natalie (aged 8). Natalie is the daughter of a mathematical logician. The family was visiting us for a weekend, and one evening we all had a lively philosophical discussion about time. For some perverse reason or other, I took the position that time is unreal.

Next morning at breakfast, someone asked of two acquaintances which was the older?

"Bill is older by two years," I remarked.

"How could he be?" asked Natalie. "Didn't you say that time was unreal?"

56

Natalie's remark reminds me of G. E. Moore's famous proof of the existence of an external world. He held up a hand and said, "Here is a hand." Then he held up his other hand and said, "Here is another hand. Hands are objects, hence objects exist."

I am also reminded of a conversation I once had with the logical positivist O. Bowsma. I took an extreme view, holding that minds were essentially independent of bodies.

"I can easily imagine myself in another body," I said. "I am fully prepared for the possibility that next week I might find myself in a totally different body, say, one with three arms."

"You are *really* prepared?" asked Bowsma.

"Absolutely!" I replied.

"Tell me," said Bowsma, "have you bought yourself another glove?"

57

As the conversation continued, I became more and more wildly idealistic. Bowsma had an objection to just about every statement I made.

"Tell me," I finally asked, "do you believe I am being inconsistent?"

"No," he replied.

Another philosopher present said, "What you are saying is too *vague* to be inconsistent!"

58

There is a curious thing about inconsistency. In the formal mathematical systems mainly in use today, consistency is absolutely essential, for without it the whole system breaks down and *everything* can be proved. It has therefore been argued that if a person is inconsistent, he will end up believing everything. But is this really so?

I have known many inconsistent people, and they don't appear to believe *everything*. First, it is difficult to live long enough to believe everything. Second, even if we were immortal and inconsistent, we would not necessarily believe everything. I say this for the following reason: If we were *consistent* in our inconsistency, then we might end up believing everything, but it is more likely that an inconsistent person would be just as inconsistent in the way he carried out his inconsistency as he is about other things, and this would be the very thing that would save him from believing everything.

The inconsistent people I have known have not seemed to have a higher ratio of false beliefs to true ones than those who make a superhuman effort to maintain consistency at all costs. True, people who are compulsively consistent will probably save themselves certain false beliefs, but I'm afraid they will also miss many true ones!

59

Here is a little paradox:

> ### YOU HAVE NO REASON
> ### TO BELIEVE THIS SENTENCE.

Do you have any reason to believe the above sentence or don't you?

60

Have you heard the business executive's paradox? It was invented by the literary agent Lisa Collier of Collier Associates. The president of a firm offered a reward of $100 to any employee who could provide a suggestion that would save the company money. One employee suggested, "Eliminate the reward!"

61

My favorite paradox of all is known as *hypergame.* It is due to the mathematician William Zwicker.

A game is called *normal* if it has to terminate in a finite number of moves. An obvious example of a normal game is tic-tac-toe. Chess is also a normal game, assuming tournament regulations. Now, the first move of hypergame is to state which normal game is to be played. For example, if you and I were playing hypergame and I had the first move, I might say, "Let's play chess." Then you make the first move in chess, and we continue playing chess until the termination of the game. Another possibility is that on my first move in hypergame, I might say, "Let's play tic-tac-toe," or "Let's play casino," or any other normal game I like. But the game I choose *must* be normal; I am not allowed to choose a game that is not normal.

The problem is, Is hypergame itself normal or not? Suppose it is normal. Since on the first move of hypergame I can choose *any* normal game, I can say, "Let's play hypergame." We are then in the state of hypergame, and it is your move. You can respond, "Let's play hypergame." I can repeat, "Let's play hypergame," and the process can go on indefinitely, contrary to the assumption that hypergame is normal. Therefore, hypergame is not a normal game. But since hypergame is not normal, on my first move in hypergame I *cannot* choose hypergame; I must choose a normal game. But having chosen a normal game, the game must finally terminate, contrary to the proven fact that hypergame is not normal.

An amazing paradox indeed!

62

A Moral Paradox. The philosopher Jaako Hintikka makes the delightful argument that one is morally obligated not to do anything impossible. The argument, which ultimately rests on the fact that a false proposition implies any proposition, is this: Suppose Act A is such that it is impossible to perform without destroying the human race. Then surely one is morally obligated not to perform that act. Well, if Act A is an *impossible* act, then it is indeed impossible to perform it without destroying the human race (since it is impossible to perform it at all!), and therefore one is morally obligated not to perform the act.

63

But doesn't the following argument *(sic!)* show that one is morally obligated to do *everything* that is impossible?

Suppose that Act B is such that if one performs it, then the human race will be saved from destruction. Isn't one then morally obligated to perform the act? Now suppose that Act B is impossible to perform. Then it *is* the case that if one performs Act B, the human race will be saved, because it is false that one will perform this impossible act and a false proposition implies anything. One is therefore morally obligated to perform every impossible act.

64

For those who like logic puzzles, here are some nice ones.

Problem 1. There are three brothers named John, Jack, and William. John and Jack always lie (make only false statements) and William makes only true statements. The three are indistinguishable in appearance. One day you meet one of the three brothers on the street and wish to know if he is John (because John owes you money). You are allowed to ask him only one question, which has to be answered by *yes* or *no*, and the question may not contain more than three words. What question would you ask? (The solutions to this and the next four problems are given in §66.)

Problem 2. Suppose in the last problem we change the conditions and make John and Jack the truth tellers and William the liar. You still want to know whether the brother you meet is John. Now what three-word question will work?

Problem 3. This time we have only two brothers. One is named John, and the other is not. One of the two always lies, and the other always tells the truth, but we don't know whether John is the liar or the truth teller. You meet both brothers together, and you wish to find out which one is John. You are allowed to ask either one of them a three-word question. What question will do the trick?

Problem 4. Suppose in the last problem you are not interested in which brother is John but only in whether John is the truthful brother or the brother who lies. What three-word question will enable you to find out?

Problem 5. I once met these two brothers on the street. I had two distinct questions in mind. I knew that if I asked the first question,

I would then know the correct answer to the second question, whereas if I asked the second question, I would then know the correct answer to the first question. Can you supply two such questions?

65

A Gödelian Machine. Of the many mathematical machines I have used to illustrate Gödel's famous proof, the following is the simplest.

The machine prints out various expressions composed of four symbols: *P,N,R,**. An expression is called *printable* if the machine can print it. A *sentence* is any expression of one of the four forms: (1) P*X; (2) NP*X; (3) PR*X; and (4) NPR*X, where X is any expression built from the four symbols. Each sentence is interpreted as follows: (1) P*X is called *true* if and only if X is printable; (2) NP*X is called *true* if and only if X is not printable (N is an abbreviation of *not,* just as P is an abbreviation of *printable*); (3) PR*X is called *true* if and only if XX is printable (XX is called the *repeat* of X, hence the letter *R*); and (4) NPR*X is called *true* if and only if XX is not printable.

We are given that the machine is completely accurate, that is, every sentence printed by the machine is a true sentence. The problem is to find a true sentence that the machine cannot print! (The solution to this problem and a discussion are given in §67.)

66

Solutions to the Puzzles of §64. For Problem 1: A question that works is, "Are you Jack?" and it is the only three-word question I can think of that does work!

Jack and William would both answer *no* to that question (Jack because he lies and William because he is truthful). John would answer *yes* (because John lies). Therefore, if you get *yes* for an answer, you will know that he is John, and if you get *no* for an answer, you will know that he is not John.

As for Problem 2: The very same question works! Only now a *yes* answer indicates that he is not John, and a *no* answer indicates that he is John.

Now, the solution to Problem 3: This is more subtle. The question, "Are you John?" is useless. Whatever answer you get could be the truth or could be a lie. A question whose correct answer you already know (such as, "Is water wet?") is no good. You will then know whether the one addressed is truthful or not, but you won't know whether or not he is John. The question, "Are you truthful?" is no good. You will get the answer *yes* from both brothers.

A question that does work is, "Is John truthful?" John would certainly claim that John is truthful (regardless of whether or not John is truthful). John's brother would claim that John is not truthful (correctly if John's brother is truthful and falsely if John's brother lies). So, a *yes* answer indicates that the one addressed is John. A *no* answer indicates that he is not John.

Another three-word question that works is, "Does John lie?" A *yes* answer to that question indicates that the one addressed is not John. A *no* answer indicates that he is John.

As for Problem 4: To find out whether John is truthful, the question, "Are you John?" now works! Suppose you get *yes* for an answer. If the speaker is truthful, then he really is John, in which case John is truthful. If the speaker is lying, then he is not John, hence John must be the truthful brother. So, whether the speaker is lying or telling the truth, a *yes* answer indicates that John is truthful. We leave it to you to verify that a *no* answer indicates that John is not truthful, regardless of whether the speaker is lying or telling the truth.

There is a pretty symmetry between the last two problems. To find out whether the one addressed is John, you ask him whether John is truthful, whereas if you want to find out whether John is truthful, you ask him whether he is John. This provides a solution to Problem 5: One question is, "Is John truthful?" The other question is, "Are you John?" Asking either question will enable you to know the correct answer, not of the question you ask, but of the other question.

67

Solution to the Gödelian Machine Puzzle. The sentence NPR*NPR* says that the repeat of NPR* is not printable (i.e., the sentence is true if and only if the repeat of NPR* is not printable). But the repeat of NPR* is the very sentence NPR*NPR*! So this sentence is true if and only if it is not printable. If the sentence is false, then it *is* printable (since the sentence says that it isn't), which would mean that the machine is capable of printing a false sentence. But we are given that the machine is accurate and never prints false sentences. So it must be that the sentence is true, hence what it says is really the case, which means that it is not printable. And so the sentence NPR*NPR* must be true, but the machine cannot print it.

The philosopher J. Michael Dunn once showed the above problem to his son, Jon. After the boy understood it, he said to his father, "One thing I would like to know. Why would anybody want to construct such a machine?" The father thought for a moment and replied, "Well, it would be nice if we could have an accurate machine that could print out all true facts about the world. But it seems that such a machine is not possible."

The whole point, of course, is that no accurate machine can possibly print a sentence that says that the machine cannot print it. In the very process of printing it the machine would falsify it! The situation is reminiscent of the scene in *Romeo and Juliet* in which the nurse comes running to Juliet and says, "I have no breath." Juliet replies, "How can you have no breath when you have breath left to say 'I have no breath'?"

68

I started this chapter with self-annihilating sentences, and it seems only fitting to end with what might aptly be called a self-annihilating conversation. The dialogue is not original. It was devised by Goodwin Sammel, a musician I first met in my University of Chicago days who has always taken an interest in mathematical matters. When he first heard about Gödel's theorem he came up with this exchange:

A: It's true!

B: It's not!

A: Yes, it is!

B: It couldn't be!

A: It *is* true!

B: Prove it!

A: Oh, it can't be proved, but nevertheless it's true.

B: Now, just a minute: How can you say it's true if it can't be proved?

A: Oh, there are certain things that are true even though they can't be proved.

B: That's not true!

A: Yes, it is; Gödel *proved* that there are certain things that are true but that cannot be proved.

B: That's not true!

A: It certainly is!

B: It couldn't be, and even if it *were* true, it could never be proved!

Notes

1. Raymond Smullyan, *What Is the Name of This Book?* (Englewood Cliffs, N.J.: Prentice-Hall, 1978), p. 208.

2. Sigmund Freud, *The Future of an Illusion* (Third edition, The International Psycho-Analytical Library #15, translated by W. D. Robson-Scott, The Hogarth Press, 37, Mecklenburgh Square, London, and the Institute of Psycho-Analysis, 1943).

3. Ambrose Bierce, *The Devil's Dictionary* (New York: Hill & Wang, 1957).

4. Douglas Hofstadter and Daniel Dennett, *The Mind's I* (New York: Basic Books, 1981).

4

A Query

I have one Catholic friend with whom I have had many a lively discussion. I once asked him which of the following two types, both of which act extremely well by Christian standards, he considered the better: The first type is sympathetic and kind by nature and acts lovingly toward his neighbor simply because he feels like it; he does not have to force himself to do so. He does not act the way he does because of any moral principle nor out of obedience to any commandments; he simply *feels* like acting as he does. By contrast, the second type, though he in fact behaves as well as the first, does not do so spontaneously but *forces* himself to do so because he believes it is the right thing to do. I asked my friend which type was the better. After thinking for a moment, he replied, "The first one sounds to me as if he is more in a state of grace, but the second one's actions have more salvation value."

An apparently similar viewpoint appears in Meister Eckhart's ninth talk of instructions, titled "How the Inclination to Sin Is Always Beneficial."[1]

Know that the impulse to wrong is never without use and benefit to the just person. Let us notice that there are two sorts of people involved. One is so constituted that he has little or no impulse to do wrong, whereas the other is often strongly tempted. His outward self is easily swayed by whatever is at hand—swayed to anger, pride, sensuality or whatever, but his better nature, his higher self, remains unmoved and will do no wrong, or be angry, or sin in any way. He therefore fights hard against whichever vice is most natural to him, as people must who are by nature choleric, proud, or otherwise weak and who will not commit the sin to which they are liable. These people are more to be praised than the first kind. Their reward is also greater and their virtue of much higher rank. For the perfection of virtue comes of struggle, or, as St. Paul says, "Virtue is made perfect in weakness."

The impulse to sin is not sin but to consent to sin, to give way to anger, is indeed sin. Surely, if a person could wish such a thing, he would not wish to be rid of the impulse to sin, for without it he would be uncertain of everything he did, doubtful about what to do, and he would miss the honor and reward of struggle and victory. Because of the impulse to evil and the excitement of it, both virtue and its rewards are in travail born. The impulse to wrong makes us the more diligent in the exercise of virtue, driving us to it with a strong hand, like a hard taskmaster, forcing us to take shelter in doing well. The weaker one is, the more he is warned to strength and self-conquest; for virtue, like vice, is a matter of the will.

Despite my general fondness for mystic writers, there are several things about the above passage that I find extremely disturbing. For one thing, certain parts are downright illogical! Is it really true that if a person had no impulse to sin he would be uncertain of everything he did and doubtful about what to do? Are saints and angels uncertain and doubtful about what to do? Aren't there other more useful and interesting things with which to occupy one's time than "exerting noble efforts to overcome one's sinful impulses"?

I think that Benjamin Franklin really hit the nail on the head in his astute essay titled "Self-Denial Not the Essence of Virtue."[2] He begins the essay as follows:

It is commonly asserted, that without self-denial there is no virtue, and that the greater the self-denial the greater the virtue.

If it were said, that he who cannot deny himself any thing he inclines to, though he knows it will be to his hurt, has not the virtue of resolution or fortitude, it would be intelligible enough; but, as it stands, it seems obscure or erroneous.

Let us consider some of the virtues singly.

If a man has no inclination to wrong people in his dealings, if he feels no temptation to it, and therefore never does it, can it be said that he is not a just man? If he is a just man, has he not the virtue of justice?

If to a certain man idle diversions have nothing in them that is tempting, and therefore he never relaxes his application to business for their sake, is he not an industrious man? Or has he not the virtue of industry?

I might in like manner instance in all the rest of the virtues; but, to make the thing short, as it is certain that the more we strive against the temptation to any vice, and practice the contrary virtue, the weaker will that temptation be, and the stronger will be that habit, till at length the temptation has no force, or entirely vanishes; does it follow from thence, that in our endeavors to overcome vice we grow continually less virtuous, till at length we have no virtue at all?

Franklin then further elaborates his point. He ends the essay with the following paragraph:

The truth is, that temperance, justice, charity &c. are virtues, whether practiced with, or against our inclinations, and the man, who practices them, merits our love and esteem; and self-denial is neither good nor bad, but as it is applied. He that denies a vicious inclination, is virtuous in proportion to his resolution; *but the most perfect virtue is above all temptation* [emphasis added]; such as the virtue of the saints in heaven; and he, who does a foolish, indecent, or wicked thing, merely because it is contrary to his inclination (like some mad enthusiasts I have read of, who ran about naked, under the notion of taking up the cross), is not practicing the reasonable science of virtue, but is a lunatic.

Notes

1.   Meister Eckhart, "How the Inclination to Sin Is Always Beneficial." In *Meister Eckhart, A Modern Translation,* Raymond Bernard Blakney (New York and London: Harper and Brothers, 1941), p. 12.

2.   Benjamin Franklin, "Self Denial Not the Essence of Virtue." In *Pennsylvania Gazette* (February 18, 1734).

3

Three Fantasies

5

Simplicus and the Tree—
An Open Air Symposium

SIMPLICUS: I am enjoying this tree.

FIRST PHILOSOPHER: No, it is not the tree you are enjoying but the *light* from the tree. It is not the tree that is directly influencing your sense organs but only its reflected light. Therefore, you are enjoying the *light* of the tree.

SECOND PHILOSOPHER: No, no, it is not the *light* he is enjoying but rather the image the light forms on his retina.

THIRD PHILOSOPHER: This is superficial physiology! The retinal image could not affect him if his optic nerves were dead, and his optic nerves are but part of his brain and nervous system. Therefore, what he is really enjoying is the neural activities of his entire brain and nervous system.

FOURTH PHILOSOPHER: I think that it is misleading to say that he is enjoying this physiological activity; I would instead say that his enjoyment of the tree *is* this physiological activity.

CARTESIAN: All of you are wrong! His physiological process is only the material counterpart of an inner mental or spiritual process; it is this spiritual soul-activity that he is enjoying.

IDEALIST: Except that the evidence for what you call the material counterpart of this mental process is, as I have demonstrated, wholly inconclusive. I don't believe in the existence of this "tree." The proper way to phrase it, therefore, is that the mind or soul of Simplicus is enjoying his idea of the tree.

IDEALISTIC MYSTIC: I deny the existence of individual minds. There is no such thing as the mind of Simplicus! There is only one universal mind, called the *world soul, cosmic consciousness, God, the Absolute,* or whatever, and it is this universal or absolute mind that is enjoying the tree, which exists as one of its ideas.

REALISTIC MYSTIC:[1]   The viewpoint of my friend the idealistic mystic is about the opposite end of the spectrum from mine, and yet it comes closer to mine—in the sense of abstract identity or isomorphism—than any other yet expressed.

I start from the premise that reality is purely material. All that exists is the material universe, which for certain purposes *might* be broken down into material particles and their motions. Simplicus's enjoyment of the tree is therefore indeed an event or set of events in the nervous system of the body of Simplicus. This viewpoint, though correct, seems to me only partial. Simplicus is not a closed physical system. When Simplicus has a thought, the particles of the cerebrum of Simplicus move not only in relation to each other but also in relation to every particle of the entire universe. I therefore wish to look upon the thoughts of Simplicus as an activity of the universe as a whole. Thus, instead of saying that it is Simplicus enjoying the tree, I would say it is the whole physical universe that is enjoying the tree.

FIRST LOGICAL POSITIVIST: I wonder if the viewpoints of the idealistic and realistic mystics really differ in content or merely in terminology. How do I know that when the first says *material* and the second *mental,* or the first *physical universe* and the second *universal mind,* that they are not merely using different words to denote the same thing?

SECOND LOGICAL POSITIVIST: I doubt that this question itself has any cognitive content. How in principle could one verify whether they mean the same or different things?

PHYSICIST: This type of question is out of my domain. I would like to return to the viewpoint of the realistic mystic. Naturally, this viewpoint interests me in that it uses the terminology of science. It has, however, one serious weakness that borders on the downright ridiculous. All right, he may translate the statement, "Simplicus enjoys the tree," to, "The universe enjoys the tree." Now suppose someone else—say, Complicus—comes along and claims to enjoy the tree. Again the mystic translates the statement, "Complicus enjoys the tree," to, "The universe enjoys the tree." So when the realistic mystic says, "The universe is enjoying the tree," how can I possibly know whether it is Simplicus, Complicus, or someone else—or for that matter some dog—who is enjoying the tree?

REALISTIC MYSTIC: I should like first to remark that by profession I am also a physicist. Now certainly, when I do physics or am engaged in daily life activities I would use the more descriptive and specific terminology, "Simplicus is enjoying the tree," or "Complicus is enjoying the tree," rather than, "The universe is enjoying the tree." Just because I regard Simplicus's enjoyment of the tree and Complicus's enjoyment of the tree as special cases of the universe enjoying the tree does not mean that I regard them as identical events. So of course when it is necessary to be more specific (which is most of the time), then I *am* specific. But for other purposes— which might be termed *spiritual, mystical,* or *religious*—I believe it more fruitful to regard these particular events as an activity of the universe as a whole.

CHRISTIAN THEOLOGIAN: Since you brought up the word *religion,* may I ask whether you honestly believe it possible to incorporate into your purely materialistic framework the fundamental ideas of religion like God, soul, divine purpose, and reward and punishment? If all that exists is matter, what could it possibly mean for my soul to be immortal, and how could I anticipate punishment or fear reward?

PSYCHIATRIST: I think you meant *fear punishment* and *anticipate reward.*

REALISTIC MYSTIC *(amused):* I certainly can incorporate all these ideas into a purely materialistic framework. By *God,* I of course mean the entire universe. The word *soul* or *mind* I happen to use most frequently. I am not a dualist in that I do not regard soul as a substance, as I do matter. Rather, *soul* for me is a combination of memories and dispositions. If I have a beautiful recording of a musical composition and the record should fall and break, it is no tragedy, providing I can get another copy. What is important about a particular record is not its particular atoms but rather the pattern that has been impressed upon it. It is this pattern that might well be called the soul of the record—its propensity to reembody the musical idea. Likewise, a man's soul consists of his memories and behavioral propensities. In this sense, it seems perfectly natural to also regard the universe as having a soul, which is its pattern. If you would prefer me to use the word *God* to mean this *soul* or *pattern* rather than its concrete embodiment, I would have no objection. After all, suppose if by magic each atom in the universe were replaced by an identical particle, or if this is empirically meaningless, suppose that all basic particles of the universe were thoroughly reshuffled but end in a pattern identical with the present one. I would hardly say that the universe had undergone any significant change; it would still have the same pattern or soul. I do, however, disagree with the idealist or dualist who thinks of soul as a substance, unless (is it possible?) he would allow a pattern to be called a substance. In this case, our difference is not metaphysical at all but purely terminological. This suggests the following thoughts on dualism versus monism.

I can see some sense in distinguishing a particular body from its pattern if there exists at least one other body with the same pattern. But since there is only one universe, it is hard to understand the difference between the universe and its pattern. This would mean that we can distinguish the mind of a man from the body of a man, or the mind of a dog from the body of a dog, but in the limiting case of God, the body of God might be the same as the mind of God. Stated in the language of the mathematician, matter and mind may be different locally but the same globally.

To return, however, to the theologian's second question, I first wish to remark that I have always found it exceedingly odd that many scientists—even those in the computer science field—are perfectly willing to use terms like *thinking, purpose, reward,* and *punishment* for both humans and computing machines but absolutely balk at the idea of applying these so-called anthropomorphic terms to the universe as a whole. Of course the universe is mainly inorganic, but so is a computer! I greatly fear that this is a sad reflection of the continuing egocentricity of mankind. Descartes thought that humans think but dogs do not. (His dog, however, thought otherwise!) People today who believe that humans think usually believe that dogs think as well. With plant life, people are doubtful, and when it comes to inorganic matter, there most people really draw the line! As if there is some social hierarchy— stones, plants, dogs, people! One calls stones *dead* and *inert.* Of course stones are dead in the purely biological sense. The word *inert* is, however, misleading, considering the fantastically rich life and activities of a stone's inner molecular structure. But to balk at applying anthropomorphic terms to the whole universe, whose structure is so vast and complex compared with any person or computer—indeed, it *includes* all people and computers—to refuse this terminology for the universe as a whole strikes me as totally unwarranted. No, I certainly have every whit as much right to apply such terms as *thinking, feeling,* and *planning* to the universe as a whole as I do to entities that are only parts of the universe. Let the tough-minded think of these terms as purely operational. My so-called mysticism consists not of any metaphysical meaning attached to this terminology but purely of my *emotional* responses that such terminology tends to engender. At any rate, in this terminology, it of course makes sense to refer to the universe as having a purpose or as punishing or rewarding us for our actions. For example, I would say that the universe punishes a baby—for its ultimate good—for sticking its hand into a fire.

As to survival after death, I have no definite opinion regarding it. In principle, there is no a priori reason why after my bodily death memories of my life may not remain in the universe and even eventuate in a reembodiment, and in principle it could be possible that I could then be rewarded or punished for my present behavior. But this is wholly speculative.

There is one aspect of religion—at least Western religion—that the theologian did not mention and that might be a bit more of a problem to incorporate into a purely materialistic framework. That is the notion that God created the universe. For this, I would need to retract my earlier statement that perhaps the mind of God is the same as the body of God. If I am allowed to distinguish the concrete universe from its abstract pattern or form, then I can certainly say that the pattern of the universe existed as a logical possibility before the universe, or better still, exists outside of time altogether. The creation of the universe by God can then simply mean the concrete embodiment of this pattern. This view may not be too far from the meaning of, "In the beginning was the Word."

CHRISTIAN THEOLOGIAN: Are you seriously advocating recasting all religion into a purely materialistic framework?

REALISTIC MYSTIC: Not at all! It is all the same to me whether religion is cast into a purely materialistic or a purely idealistic or a dualistic framework. I do not advocate any one more than any other. Personally, I happen to think in materialistic terms, though I am not a nominalist since my ontology does indeed include abstract entities like forms and patterns. My main point now is not that religion *should* be cast in materialist terms but only that it *can* be. My whole claim is that the kernel of religion—that part of religion that is of chief ethical and psychological significance—is totally neutral with respect to any metaphysical foundations.

FIRST EPISTEMOLOGIST: Enough theology! Let us come to a *practical* question. How does Simplicus *know* that he is enjoying the tree?

SECOND EPISTEMOLOGIST: Simplicus never said that he *knew* that he was enjoying the tree but only that he *was* enjoying the tree.

FIRST EPISTEMOLOGIST: But *does* Simplicus know that he is enjoying the tree?

SECOND EPISTEMOLOGIST: I don't know.

FIRST EPISTEMOLOGIST: How do you know you don't know?

SECOND EPISTEMOLOGIST: I don't.

FIRST EPISTEMOLOGIST: Then how do I know that Simplicus does know that he is enjoying the tree? For all I know, maybe he doesn't know that he is enjoying the tree.

RABBI: All right, so maybe he doesn't know he is enjoying the tree!

FIRST MEANY:[2]   I don't believe in fact that Simplicus *is* enjoying the tree!

SECOND MEANY: Exactly! The very fact that he says he is only proves that he isn't.

THIRD MEANY: Yeah, if he were really enjoying it, he would not have to say he was. When someone really enjoys something, he does not have to broadcast it to the world. When Simplicus says, "I am enjoying this tree," methinks the gentleman doth protest too much.

MORALIST: No, no, Simplicus obviously *is* enjoying the tree—just look at his face! What I question is whether he has the *right* to enjoy the tree!

SECOND MORALIST: Exactly! With all the starvation, misery, and social injustice in the world, what the hell is Simplicus doing there sitting under the tree when he should be out in the world helping matters?

ZEN MASTER: All this metaphysics, theology, epistemology, and ethics is certainly of interest, but do any of you here really think you have cast the faintest ray of light on the meaning of Simplicus's original statement? When Simplicus says, "I am enjoying the tree," it means nothing more or less than that Simplicus is enjoying the tree.[3] All of you have made the tacit but wholly unwarranted assumption that this statement expresses a relation between some subject and some object. Everyone has been discussing who has done what to whom, that is, what it was that was enjoyed and who it really was that was doing the enjoying. Can't you simply accept Simplicus's enjoyment of the tree as an event that is nonanalyzable? Every sentence when translated loses its essential meaning. The sentence, "Simplicus is enjoying the tree," simply means that Simplicus is enjoying the tree.

ZEN STUDENT: My master is right! The simple truth is that there is no Simplicus to enjoy and no tree to be enjoyed. In reality, there is just this one unanalyzable event of Simplicus enjoying the tree. This event is not a relation but just an occurrence in the great void!

ZEN MASTER *(slugging the novice):*   Oh, you great little snit! You the "enlightened one" know all about simple truth, reality, and the great void, don't you? And it is up to you to enlighten all these "poor ignorant" people with your great newfound wisdom, eh?

ZEN STUDENT: But master, how else can I get these people to understand the *essence* of Simplicus's statement?

ZEN MASTER *(giving him another blow):*   By holding your tongue! Damn it all, how many times must I tell you that there is no *essence* to be understood! If these people can't understand the perfectly plain statement, "I am enjoying this tree," then perhaps a few blows with my stick might enlighten them!

SECOND ZEN MASTER: I think everyone here should be given a blow with the stick regardless of whether he understands Simplicus's statement or not.

THIRD ZEN MASTER: Better still, I think everyone should be given a nonblow with a nonstick.

MORALIST *(in great alarm):*   This psychotic conversation has gone far enough! Unless this stops immediately, *and I mean immediately,* I will get very angry, and when I get angry, I can become *very* unpleasant!

SIMPLICUS: But the tree is so beautiful, why shouldn't I enjoy it?

Notes

1. I do not know if there is a school of thought called *realistic mysticism;* if not, let this be the beginning of one.

2. I obtained the term *meany* from the Beatles's movie *Yellow Submarine,* in which the villains were called *blue meanies.*

3. Shades of Alfred Tarski!

6

An Epistemological Nightmare

Scene 1. Frank is in the office of an eye doctor. The doctor holds up a book and asks, "What color is it?" Frank answers, "Red." The doctor says, "Aha, just as I thought! Your whole color mechanism has gone out of kilter. But fortunately your condition is curable, and I will have you in perfect shape in a couple of weeks."

Scene 2 (a few weeks later). Frank is in the laboratory of an experimental epistemologist. *(You will soon find out what that means!)* The epistemologist holds up a book and also asks, "What color is it?" Now, Frank has been earlier dismissed by the eye doctor as "cured," but he is now of a very analytical and cautious temperament and will not make any statement that can possibly be refuted. So Frank answers, "It seems red to me."

EPISTEMOLOGIST: Wrong!

FRANK: I don't think you heard what I said. I merely said that it *seems* red to me.

EPISTEMOLOGIST: I heard you, and you were wrong.

FRANK: Let me get this clear; do you mean that I was wrong that this book *is* red or that I was wrong that it *seems* red to me?

EPISTEMOLOGIST: I obviously couldn't have meant that you were wrong that it *is* red since you did not say that it is red. All you said was that it *seems* red to you, and it is *this* statement that is wrong.

FRANK: But you can't say that the statement, "It *seems* red to me," is wrong.

EPISTEMOLOGIST: If I *can't* say it, how come I did?

FRANK: I mean you can't *mean* it.

EPISTEMOLOGIST: Why not?

FRANK: But surely *I* know what color the book *seems* to me!

EPISTEMOLOGIST: Again you are wrong.

FRANK: But nobody knows better than I how things seem to *me*.

EPISTEMOLOGIST: I am sorry, but again you are wrong.

FRANK: But who knows better than I?

EPISTEMOLOGIST: I do.

FRANK: But how could you have access to my private mental states?

EPISTEMOLOGIST: Private mental states! Metaphysical hogwash! Look, I am a *practical* epistemologist. Metaphysical problems about mind versus matter arise only from epistemological confusions. Epistemology is the true foundation of philosophy, but the trouble with all past epistemologists is that they have been using wholly theoretical methods, and much of their discussion degenerates into mere word games. While other epistemologists have been solemnly arguing such questions as whether a man can be wrong when he asserts that he believes such and such, I have discovered how to settle such questions *experimentally*.

FRANK: How could you possibly decide such things empirically?

EPISTEMOLOGIST: By reading a person's thoughts directly.

FRANK: You mean you are telepathic?

EPISTEMOLOGIST: Of course not. I simply did the one obvious thing that should be done: I have constructed a brain-reading machine—

known technically as a *cerebrescope*—that is operative right now in this room and is scanning every nerve cell in your brain. I thus can read your every sensation and thought, and it is a simple objective truth that this book does *not* seem red to you.

FRANK *(thoroughly subdued):*   Goodness gracious, I really could have sworn that the book seemed red to me; it sure *seems* that it seems red to me!

EPISTEMOLOGIST: I'm sorry, but you are wrong again.

FRANK: Really? It doesn't even *seem* that it seems red to me? It sure *seems* that it seems that it seems red to me!

EPISTEMOLOGIST: Wrong again! And no matter how many times you reiterate the phrase *it seems that* and follow it by *the book is red,* you will be wrong.

FRANK: This is fantastic! Suppose instead of the phrase *it seems that,* I said *I believe that.* So let us start again at ground level. I retract the statement, "It seems red to me," and instead I assert, "I *believe* that this book is red." Is this statement true or false?

EPISTEMOLOGIST: Just a moment while I scan the dials of the brain-reading machine—no, your statement is false.

FRANK: What about, "I believe that I believe that the book is red"?

EPISTEMOLOGIST *(consulting his dials):*   Also false. And again, no matter how many times you reiterate *I believe,* all these belief sentences are false.

FRANK: Well, this has been a most enlightening experience. You must admit, however, that it is a *little* hard on me to realize that I am entertaining infinitely many erroneous beliefs!

EPISTEMOLOGIST: Why do you say that your beliefs are erroneous?

FRANK: But you have been telling me this all the while!

EPISTEMOLOGIST: I most certainly have not!

FRANK: Good God, I was prepared to admit all my errors and now you tell me that my beliefs are *not* errors; what are you trying to do, drive me crazy?

EPISTEMOLOGIST: Hey, take it easy! Please try to recall: When did I say or imply that any of your beliefs are erroneous?

FRANK: Just simply recall the infinite sequence of sentences: (1) I believe that this book is red; (2) I believe that I believe that this book is red; and so forth. You told me that every one of those statements is false.

EPISTEMOLOGIST: True.

FRANK: Then how can you consistently maintain that my *beliefs* in all these false statements are not erroneous?

EPISTEMOLOGIST: Because, as I told you, you don't believe any of them.

FRANK: I think I see, yet I am not absolutely sure.

EPISTEMOLOGIST: Look, let me put it another way. Don't you see that the very falsity of each of the statements that you assert *saves* you from an erroneous belief in the preceding one? The first statement is, as I told you, false. Very well! Now the second statement simply says that you believe the first statement. If the second statement were *true*, then you would believe the first statement, and hence your belief about the first statement would indeed be in error. But fortunately the second statement is false, so you don't really believe the first statement; your belief in the first statement is therefore not in error. Thus, the falsity of the second statement implies that you do *not* have an erroneous belief about the first; the falsity of the third likewise saves you from an erroneous belief about the second; and so forth.

FRANK: Now I see perfectly! So none of my *beliefs* was erroneous, only the statements were erroneous.

EPISTEMOLOGIST: Exactly.

FRANK: Most remarkable! Incidentally, what color is the book really?

EPISTEMOLOGIST: It is red.

FRANK: What!

EPISTEMOLOGIST: Exactly! Of course the book is red. What's the matter with you, don't you have eyes?

FRANK: But didn't I in effect keep saying that the book is red all along?

EPISTEMOLOGIST: Of course not! You kept saying it *seems* red to you, it *seems* that it seems red to you, you *believe* it is red, you *believe* that you believe it is red, and so forth. Not once did you say that it *is* red. When I asked you originally, "What color is the book?" if you had simply answered, "Red," this whole painful discussion would have been avoided.

Scene 3. Frank comes back several months later to the laboratory of the epistemologist.

EPISTEMOLOGIST: How delightful to see you! Please sit down.

FRANK *(seated)*:   I have been thinking much of our last discussion, and there is much I wish to clear up. To begin with, I discovered an inconsistency in some of the things you said.

EPISTEMOLOGIST: Delightful! I love inconsistencies. Pray tell!

FRANK: Well, you claimed that although my belief sentences were false, I did not have any actual *beliefs* that are false. If you had not admitted that the book actually is red, you would have been' consistent. But your very admission that the book *is* red leads to an inconsistency.

EPISTEMOLOGIST: How so?

FRANK: Look, as you correctly pointed out, in each of my belief sentences, "I believe that it is red," "I believe that I believe that it is red," and so forth, the falsity of each one other than the first saves me from an erroneous belief in the preceding one. You neglected, however, to take into consideration the first sentence itself! The falsity of the first sentence, "I believe that it is red," in conjunction with the fact that it *is* red, *does* imply that I have a false belief.

EPISTEMOLOGIST: I don't see why.

FRANK: It is obvious! Since the sentence, "I believe it is red," is false, then I in fact believe it is not red, and since it really is red, then I *do* have a false belief. So there!

EPISTEMOLOGIST *(disappointed):* I am sorry, but your proof obviously fails. Of course the falsity of the fact that you believe it is red implies that you *don't* believe it is red. But this does not mean that you believe it is *not* red!

FRANK: But obviously I know that either it is red or it isn't, so if I don't believe that it is, then I must believe that it isn't.

EPISTEMOLOGIST: Not at all. I believe that either Jupiter has life or it doesn't. But I neither believe that it does nor do I believe that it doesn't. I have no evidence one way or the other.

FRANK: I guess you are right. But let us come to more important matters. I honestly find it impossible that I can be in error concerning my own beliefs.

EPISTEMOLOGIST: Must we go through this again? I have already patiently explained to you that you (in the sense of your beliefs, not your statements) are *not* in error.

FRANK: Oh, all right then, I simply do not believe that even the *statements* are in error. Yes, according to the machine, they are in error, but why should I trust the machine?

EPISTEMOLOGIST: Whoever said that you should trust the machine?

FRANK: Well, *should* I trust the machine?

EPISTEMOLOGIST: That question involving the word *should* is out of my domain. However, if you like, I can refer you to a colleague who is an excellent moralist—he may be able to answer this for you.

FRANK: Oh, come on now, I obviously didn't mean *should* in a moralistic sense. I simply meant, "Do I have any evidence that this machine is reliable?"

EPISTEMOLOGIST: Well, do you?

FRANK: Don't ask *me!* What I mean is, Should *you* trust the machine?

EPISTEMOLOGIST: *Should* I trust it? I have no idea, and I couldn't care less what I *should* do.

FRANK: Oh, your moralistic hang-up again. I mean, Do *you* have evidence that the machine is reliable?

EPISTEMOLOGIST: Well of course!

FRANK: Then let us get down to brass tacks. What is your evidence?

EPISTEMOLOGIST: You hardly can expect that I can answer this question for you in an hour, a day, or even a week. If you wish to study this machine with me, we can do so, but I assure you that this is a matter of several years. At the end of that time, however, you would certainly not have the slightest doubts about the reliability of the machine.

FRANK: Well, possibly I could believe that it is reliable in the sense that its measurements are accurate, but then I would doubt that what it actually measures is very significant. It seems that all it measures is one's physiological states and activities.

EPISTEMOLOGIST: But of course, what else would you expect it to measure?

FRANK: I doubt that it measures my psychological states, my actual *beliefs.*

EPISTEMOLOGIST: Are we back to that again? The machine *does* measure those physiological states and processes, which you call psychological states, beliefs, sensations, and so forth.

FRANK: At this point, I am becoming convinced that our entire difference is purely semantical. All right, I will grant that your machine does correctly measure beliefs in *your* sense of the word *belief,* but I don't believe that it can possibly measure beliefs in *my* sense of the word. In other words, I claim that our entire deadlock is simply the result of our meaning different things by the word *belief.*

EPISTEMOLOGIST: Fortunately, the correctness of your claim can be experimentally decided. It so happens that I now have two brain-reading machines in my office, so I now direct one to *your* brain to find out what *you* mean by *belief* and the other to my own brain to find out what *I* mean by *belief*, and I shall compare the two readings. Nope, I'm sorry, but it turns out that we mean *exactly* the same thing by the word *belief*.

FRANK: Oh, hang your machine! Do *you* believe we mean the same thing by the word *belief?*

EPISTEMOLOGIST: Do *I* believe it? Just a moment while I check with the machine. Yes, it turns out that I do believe it.

FRANK: My goodness, do you mean to say that you can't even tell me what *you* believe without consulting the machine?

EPISTEMOLOGIST: Of course not.

FRANK: But most people when asked what they believe simply *tell* you. Why do you, to find out your beliefs, go through the fantastically roundabout process of directing a brain-reading machine to your own brain and then finding out what you believe on the basis of the machine's readings?

EPISTEMOLOGIST: What other scientific, objective way is there of finding out what I believe?

FRANK: Oh come now, why don't you just ask yourself?

EPISTEMOLOGIST *(sadly):*   It doesn't work. Whenever I ask myself what I believe, I never get any answer!

FRANK: Well, why don't you just *state* what you believe?

EPISTEMOLOGIST: How can I state what I believe before I know what I believe?

FRANK: Oh, to hell with your *knowledge* of what you believe; surely you have some *idea* or *belief* as to what you believe, don't you?

EPISTEMOLOGIST: Of course I have such a belief. But how do I find out what this belief is?

FRANK: I am afraid we are getting into another infinite regression. Look, at this point I am honestly beginning to wonder whether you may be going crazy.

EPISTEMOLOGIST: Let me consult the machine. Yes, it turns out that I may be going crazy.

FRANK: Good God, man, doesn't this frighten you?

EPISTEMOLOGIST: Let me check! Yes, it turns out that it does frighten me.

FRANK: Oh please, can't you forget this damned machine and just tell me whether you are frightened or not?

EPISTEMOLOGIST: I just told you that I am. However, I only learned of this from the machine.

FRANK: I can see that it is utterly hopeless to wean you away from the machine. Very well, then, let us play along with the machine some more. Why don't you ask the machine whether your sanity can be saved?

EPISTEMOLOGIST: Good idea! Yes, it turns out that it can be saved.

FRANK: And how can it be saved?

EPISTEMOLOGIST: I don't know, I haven't asked the machine.

FRANK: Well, for God's sake, ask it!

EPISTEMOLOGIST: Good idea. It turns out that . . .

FRANK: It turns out what?

EPISTEMOLOGIST: It turns out that . . .

FRANK: Come on now, it turns out what?

EPISTEMOLOGIST: This is the most fantastic thing I have ever come across! According to the machine, the best thing I can do is to cease to trust the machine!

FRANK: Good! What will you do about it?

EPISTEMOLOGIST: How do I know what I *will* do about it; I can't read the future!

FRANK: I mean, What do you *presently* intend to do about it?

EPISTEMOLOGIST: Good question, let me consult the machine. According to the machine, my present intentions are in complete conflict. And I can see why! I am caught in a terrible paradox! If the machine is trustworthy, then I had better accept its suggestion to distrust it. But if I distrust it, then I must also distrust its suggestion to distrust it, so I am really in a total quandary.

FRANK: Look, I know someone who I think might really be of help in this problem. I shall leave you for a while to consult him. Until then, *au revoir!*

Scene 4 (later in the day at a psychiatrist's office).

FRANK: Doctor, I am terribly worried about a friend of mine. He calls himself an *experimental epistemologist.*

DOCTOR: Oh, the experimental epistemologist. There is only one in the world. I know him well!

FRANK: That is a relief. But do you realize that he has constructed a brain-reading device that he now directs to his own brain, and whenever one asks him what he thinks, believes, feels, fears, and so forth, he has to first consult the machine before answering? Don't you think this is pretty serious?

DOCTOR: Not as serious as it might seem. My prognosis for him is actually quite good.

FRANK: Well, if you are a friend of his, couldn't you sort of keep an eye on him?

DOCTOR: I do see him quite frequently, and I do observe him, but I don't think that he can be helped by so-called psychiatric treatment. His problem is an unusual one and is the sort that has to work itself out. And I believe it will.

FRANK: Well, I hope your optimism is justified. At any rate, I sure think that *I* need some help at this point!

DOCTOR: How so?

FRANK: My experiences with the epistemologist have been thoroughly unnerving! At this point, I wonder if *I* may be going crazy; I can't even have confidence in how things *appear* to me. I think maybe *you* could be helpful here.

DOCTOR: I would be happy to help but cannot for awhile. For the next three months, I am unbelievably overloaded with work. After that, I unfortunately must go on a three-month vacation. So in six months, come back and we can talk this over.

Scene 5 (same office, six months later).

DOCTOR: Before we go into your problems, you will be happy to hear that your friend the epistemologist is now completely recovered.

FRANK: Marvelous! How did it happen?

DOCTOR: Almost, as it were, by a stroke of fate—and yet his very mental activities were, so to speak, part of the "fate." What happened was this. For months after you last saw him, he went around worrying, Should he trust the machine, shouldn't he trust the machine, should he, shouldn't he, should he, shouldn't he? (He decided to use the word *should* in your empirical sense.) He got nowhere! So he then decided to formalize the whole argument. He reviewed his study of symbolic logic, took the axioms of first order logic, and added as nonlogical axioms certain relevant facts about the machine. Of course, the resulting system was inconsistent—he formally proved that he should trust the machine if and only if he shouldn't and hence that he both should and should not trust the machine. Now, as you may know, in a system based on classical logic (which is the logic he used), if one can prove so much as a single contradictory proposition, then one can prove any proposition, hence the whole system breaks down. So he decided to use a logic close to what is known as *minimal logic* that is weaker than classical logic. In this weaker logic the proof of one contradiction does not necessarily entail the proof of every proposition. However, this system turned out to be too weak to decide the question of whether or not he should trust the machine. Then he had the following bright idea. Why not use classical logic in his system even though the resulting system is inconsistent? Is an inconsistent system necessarily useless? Not at all! Even though, given any proposition, there exists a proof that it is true and another proof that it is false, it may be the case that for any such pair of proofs, one of them is simply more psychologically convincing than the other, so simply pick the proof that you actually believe! Theoretically, the idea turned out very well—the actual system he obtained really did have the property that, given any such pair of proofs, one of them was always psychologically *far* more convincing than the other. Better yet, given any pair of contra-dictory propositions, *all* proofs of one were more convincing than *any* proof of the other. Indeed, anyone *except the epistemologist* could have used the system to decide whether the machine could be trusted. But the epistemologist obtained one proof that he should trust the machine, and another proof that he should not. Which proof was more convincing to him, which proof did he really believe? The only way that *he* could find out was to consult the machine! But he realized that this would be begging the question, since his con-sulting the machine would be a tacit admission that he did in fact trust the machine. So he still remained in a quandary.

FRANK: So how did he get out of it?

DOCTOR: Here is where fate kindly interceded. Because of his abso-lute absorption in the theory of this problem, which consumed almost all his waking hours, he became for the first time in his life experimentally negligent. As a result, a few minor units of his ma-chine blew out without his knowing! Then, for the first time, the machine started giving contradictory information—not merely sub-tle paradoxes but blatant contradictions. In particular, the machine claimed one day that the epistemologist believed a certain proposi-tion, and a few days later claimed that he did *not* believe that proposition. To add insult to injury, the machine claimed that he had not changed his belief in the last few days. This was enough to make him totally distrust the machine. Now he is fit as a fiddle.

FRANK: This is certainly the most amazing thing I have ever heard! I guess the machine was really dangerous and unreliable all along.

DOCTOR: Oh, not at all; the machine used to be excellent before the epistemologist's experimental carelessness put it out of whack.

FRANK: Well, surely when *I* knew it, it couldn't have been very reliable.

DOCTOR: Not so, Frank, and this brings us to your problem. I know about your entire conversation with the epistemologist. It was all tape-recorded.

FRANK: Then surely you realize that the machine could not have been right when it denied that I *believed* the book was red.

DOCTOR: Why not?

FRANK: Good God, do I have to go through all this nightmare again? I can understand that a person can be wrong if he claims that a certain physical object has a certain property, but have you ever known a single case in which a person can be mistaken when he claims to have or not have a certain sensation?

DOCTOR: Why, certainly! I once knew a Christian Scientist who had a raging toothache; he was frantically groaning and moaning all over the place. When asked whether a dentist might not cure him, he replied that there was nothing to be cured. Then he was asked, "But do you not feel pain?" He replied, "No, I do not feel pain; nobody feels pain, there is no such thing as pain, pain is only an illusion." So here is a case of a man who claimed not to feel pain, yet everyone present knew perfectly well that he did feel pain. I certainly don't believe that he was lying; he was simply mistaken.

FRANK: Well, all right in a case like that. But how can one be mistaken if one asserts his belief about the color of a book?

DOCTOR: I can assure you that, without access to any machine, if I asked someone the color of a book and he answered, "I believe that it is red," I would be very doubtful that he really believed it. It seems to me that if he really believed it, he would answer, "It is red," and not, "I believe that it is red," or, "It seems red to me." The very timidity of his response would be indicative of his doubts.

FRANK: But why on earth should I have doubted that it was red?

DOCTOR: You should know that better than I. Let us see now, have you ever in the past had reason to doubt the accuracy of your sense perception?

FRANK: Why, yes. A few weeks before visiting the epistemologist, I suffered from an eye disease, which did make me see colors falsely. But I was cured before my visit.

DOCTOR: Oh, so no wonder you doubted that it was red! True enough, your eyes perceived the correct color of the book, but your earlier experience lingered in your mind and made it impossible for you to really believe that it was red. So the machine *was* right!

FRANK: Well, all right, but then why did I doubt that I *believed* it was red?

DOCTOR: Because you *didn't* believe that it was red, and you were unconsciously smart enough to realize that. Besides, when one starts doubting one's own sense perceptions, the doubt spreads like an infection to higher and higher levels of abstraction until finally the whole belief system becomes one doubting mass of insecurity. I bet that if you went *now* to the epistemologist's office, and if the machine were repaired, and you now claimed that you believe the book is red, the machine would concur.

No, Frank, the machine is—or rather was—a good one. The epistemologist learned much from it but misused it when he applied it to his own brain. He really should have known better than to create such an unstable situation. The combination of his brain and the machine each scrutinizing and influencing the behavior of the other led to serious problems in feedback. Finally, the whole system went into a cybernetic wobble. Something was bound to give sooner or later. Fortunately, it was the machine.

FRANK: I see. One last question, though. How could the machine be trustworthy when it claimed to be untrustworthy?

DOCTOR: The machine never claimed to be untrustworthy, it only claimed that the epistemologist would be better off not trusting it. And the machine was right.

7

A Mind-Body Fantasy

In Rudolf Carnap's article "Psychology in Physical Language," he argues that every sentence of psychology may be formulated in physical language.[1] As he expresses it, all sentences of psychology describe physical occurrences, namely, the physical behavior of humans and other animals.

I do not see that the second formulation is really implied by the first. It may indeed be perfectly possible that every statement in psychology may be *translatable* into a statement in physics. But this does not mean that statements in psychology are *about* physical occurrences. The following analogy will, I hope, add some insight into this point.

Imagine (if you can!) a world with the very curious property that any two objects have the same color if and only if they happen to have the same shape. So, for instance, all red objects are spherical and all spherical objects red; all green objects are cubical and all cubical objects green; and so forth. Imagine also that half the inhabitants of the world are completely color-blind, and the other half see colors perfectly. In this world, *color* is the analogue of *mental* and *shape* is the analogue of *physical.* Hence, the materialists are the color-blind, and the dualists are the color-sighted. (Unfortunately, I cannot fit pure idealists into this world, for who could they be other than people who could see colors but not shapes—and this is too outlandish even for me!)

Imagine the metaphysical controversies that might rage on such a planet! The color-sighted people would claim certainty that objects could differ not only in size and shape but also by something else equally important, which they called *color;* they would claim to know this by direct perception and not through any process of reasoning! The color-blind people would be completely skeptical; they would consider the views of the color-sighted occult or mystical, and with good reason! In this setup, the color-sighted people would have absolutely no way of demonstrating their color-vision to the color-blind! Whenever a color-sighted person could distinguish two objects by their color-difference, a color-blind person could just as well distinguish them by their difference in shape. So no empirical demonstration to the color-blind would be possible. Also, in this setup, all statements about colors would be translatable into statements about shapes (at least in the opinion of the color-blind!). Now suppose that the color-sighted developed a dual vocabulary employing both color-words and shape-words. (I will consider some objections to this dual vocabulary later.) Half the words of this vocabulary would be redundant to the color-blind. A color-sighted person would say, "This object is both spherical *and* red, which is saying two very different things about it." The color-blind person would reply, "I still cannot understand your distinction between the words *spherical* and *red.*" Imagine the theories that the color-sighted people might invent to account for the dual phenomena of shape and color! Some might regard shape and color as different aspects or modes of the same underlying substance. Others might marvel that God has preordained some miraculous harmony between shapes and colors. Then there would arise an identity theory that would maintain that despite the possible difference between the meanings of the words *color* and *shape,* colors and shapes themselves were nevertheless the same things. Of course, the color-blind people would have no idea what the metaphysicians were talking about.

Naturally, one can easily pick my analogy to pieces. For one thing, it could be asked, "What happens if a red sphere is cut into two hemispheres; do the two halves suddenly change color?" Of course they would have to in such a world! How? By some weird physical law or other. Also, in such a world, there could be no two sources of different monochromatic lights—let's say there was only a constant source of white light. Many other utter implausibilities would have to be explained, but the point is not whether such a world is remotely realistic *or even logically possible;* this is only an analogy whose purpose is (I hope) to provide some feeling for certain aspects of the mind-body problem.

There are, however, even more fundamentally serious difficulties with this analogy. In the first place, why should the color-sighted have ever developed a dual vocabulary? Next, how could the color-sighted have ever known that the others were color-blind? For that matter, how could a color-sighted person test someone else to find out whether or not he had color-vision? And for *that* matter, could anyone know whether *he* could see colors or not? In fact, could any distinction at all between colors and shapes ever have arisen; could these two different notions have developed?

I think that this question is highly important, but I do not claim to know the answer. I suspect that the answer is, "Yes, they would," but, curiously enough, by analogy with the mind-body problem. Let us for the moment assume there is a perfect parallelism between mental and physical events. Nevertheless, some people on this earth —perhaps the majority—do indeed make a radical distinction between the two and strongly claim that these are two very different notions, not one.

Of course, one way that color-shape distinctions could arise on this planet would be if some of the color-sighted inhabitants had come from a neighboring planet on which the optical and physical laws were like those on Earth. These few would have made a sharp distinction between color and shape *prior* to having landed on this strange planet. Imagine their utter surprise! Could they, do you think, be able to test the others for color-vision? Perhaps only by taking them back to their home planet!

I'd now like to consider a slightly frightening variant of our analogy. Again, our Planet *A* is such that any two objects have the same shape if and only if they have the same color. Again, half the people are color-sighted—by which I mean that they have that physiological equipment which those of us have who can see colors—and the other half are color-blind. Let us assume now that in fact *nobody* on the planet had ever suspected that there was any difference between colors and shapes and that the color-sighted people had no idea that they were any different from the color-blind. Furthermore, only one vocabulary had developed; let us say that *spherical* was used to mean both spherical and red (which are coextensive); cubical meant both cubical and green; and so forth.

Now suppose a band from that planet were to travel for the first time to another planet—a normal planet like Earth. Imagine the reactions of the color-sighted. They might well think that they were going crazy! They would see, let us say, a red, spherical Object *A*, a green, spherical Object *B*, and a green, cubical Object *C*. Objects *A* and *C* would be perfectly normal. But Object *B*! What kind of a hybrid monster is this! Imagine how they would try to describe it back home! "It is both spherical *and* cubical!" (By which, of course, they would mean, "It is both spherical and green.")

"What do you mean by this nonsense? How can something be both spherical and cubical?"

"Well, in one way it is spherical; in another way it is cubical."

"Oh, come on now, what kind of mystical, dialectical nonsense is this? We all know that the statement, 'A spherical object is not cubical,' is analytic—it is *necessarily* true."

"Well, in one sense it is analytic, but in another sense it is actually false."

And so forth.

If the travelers remained on the other planet for awhile, they would, of course, have to develop a dual vocabulary. When they returned home, they would then realize the distinction between color-vision and shape-perception. Would you say that they had had color-vision all along but didn't know it? (Perhaps this is similar to the belief of certain Eastern mystics that all of us are already in a state of enlightenment but don't yet know it!) Some readers will probably say, "Yes, they always had it," others, "No, they did not," and still others (who are positivistically oriented) that the question is meaningless unless it means that they had the potential to distinguish differently colored objects of the same size and shape on a normal planet. I believe, though, that after returning home most of the travelers would have said, "Yes, I had color-vision all along, but I did not realize it. I have not *gained* any new faculty, I merely have become aware of a certain faculty I always possessed." (Perhaps this is again not too far removed from what is meant by certain Zen-enlightened people who have claimed, "From enlightenment I have *gained* nothing.")

I hope my reader will at least *feel* some analogy to the mind-body problem. What baffles me most about this problem is how it is that we disagree among ourselves so radically about such a basic question! Dualists do not talk about sensations as opposed to physical events, as something occult or unknown but as something known directly and with absolute certainty. Monistic materialists claim this notion to be illusory, occult, or mystical, as are the notions of minds or souls. Why this fantastic difference? No amount of deductive or inductive reasoning ever seems to settle it! So, to what can the difference be attributed? I hardly can believe that the dualists have some extra *perceptive* faculty (like color-vision) that the materialists lack! Is it possible that settling the difference will take something as drastic as the discovery one day of a *lack* of parallelism between mental and physical phenomena?

Notes

1.   Rudolf Carnap, "Psychology in Physical Language." In *Logical Positivism*, edited by A. J. Ayer (New York: The Free Press, 1966) p. 165.

4

To Be or Not to Be?

8

To Be or Not to Be?

I once posed the question, "What is the difference between an optimist and an incurable optimist?" Answer: "An optimist is one who says, "Everything is for the best; mankind will survive." An incurable optimist is one who says, "Everything is for the best; mankind will survive. And even if mankind doesn't survive, it is still for the best."

Then there is the pessimistic optimist who sadly shakes his head and says, "I'm very much afraid that everything is for the best." I think that the philosopher Arthur Schopenhauer can best be characterized as an optimistic pessimist. He happily and proudly nods his head and says, "See, everything is still for the worst," and he is optimistic that things will continue going as badly as he predicts.

Although Schopenhauer is usually called a pessimist, he can hardly be said to have a truly tragic sense of life, as have such writers as Leopardi or Unamuno. No, he has rather an *angry* sense of life. William James really hit the nail on the head when he said that Schopenhauer reminds one of a barking dog who would rather have the world ten times worse than it is than lose his chance of barking at it. It is indeed true that Schopenhauer is least convincing as a pessimist when he is most petulant.

I think a distinction should be made between what might be termed *essential pessimism* and *contingent pessimism*. I would define *essential pessimism* as the belief that life *has* to be predominantly painful, even under the best possible circumstances. By *contingent pessimism*, I mean the doctrine that as a matter of fact life is predominantly painful, but there is no a priori reason that it has to be. Thus, a contingent pessimist would say that this world is a pretty rotten one (and will likely remain so), but there is no logical necessity for this to be. Whereas essential pessimism leaves no hope for life at all, contingent pessimism leaves room for some hope, though perhaps only a slim one. It should be noted that the existence of only one predominantly happy life would constitute a disproof of essential pessimism but not of contingent pessimism.

Schopenhauer kept mixing up the two in a rather confusing way. I think that if he had left out his contingent pessimism, his essential pessimism would have come through more convincingly. As an essential pessimist, he tried to make the point that as soon as one desire is gratified, another one arises, and so the individual is as unhappy as before. As a contingent pessimist he kept ranting and raving about such things as how mendacious and hypocritical people are. But if Schopenhauer's essential pessimism is correct, why should these issues even matter? If people became less mendacious and hypocritical, how would that solve the real problem, which is life itself?

Von Hartmann. Now, the philosopher Eduard von Hartmann (a successor of Schopenhauer) strikes me as much more interesting. I am amazed that his book *Philosophy of the Unconscious* is not more widely known today than it is. His philosophical system is as wild as anything found in science fiction.

To begin with, he is far more convincing than Schopenhauer. He does not seem to take a perverse delight in how bad things are but instead seems genuinely concerned about what can be done to help matters. He has none of Schopenhauer's hysteria. His writings are completely sober, which adds to the convincing quality. He is far more an essential pessimist than a contingent one. He first sets out to dispel what he considers the three main illusions of mankind:

(1) That life is not really all that bad; (2) that there is an afterlife in which we will be happy; and (3) that through science and progress the world can be improved.

After many, many arguments to dispel these illusions, he considers the question, In virtue of all this, why shouldn't we commit suicide? He rightfully rejects Schopenhauer's silly reason that we would then never have the satisfaction of knowing we had done it. So why shouldn't we commit suicide for von Hartmann? It is because he believed that we are all but parts of one vast universal unconscious (gradually becoming conscious through evolutionary processes). We are but limbs of a single tree. Thus, if one individual commits suicide, the general problem would not be helped. What if we all committed suicide? No good. The collective unconscious that has come to life once would surely come to life again and suffer as much as before.

Then what *should* we do? Answer: We should develop science and cooperate with the spirit of progress as much as possible. Why? To make the world a happier place? No. This cannot be done, as the author has already argued. The real reason we should cooperate with science and progress is to aid evolution in accomplishing its true end. What is this end? Why, the entire purpose of evolution is that the collective unconscious develop enough knowledge to find a way of annihilating itself in such a manner that it can *never* come back!

This, in a nutshell, is von Hartmann's system. Wouldn't it be funny if it were correct?

I once asked the philosopher Bowsma why it was that when I read the pessimistic philosophers, instead of getting depressed, I feel enormously cheered up. He replied, "Of course, because you know it isn't true!" I'm not sure that this is quite the reason; it may be so for Schopenhauer, whose arguments are so unconvincing (in a way almost fraudulent). But von Hartmann seems so utterly earnest and sincere that it is hardly possible not to take him seriously. Of course, he may well be wrong in any or all of his fundamental theses. It may be that present life is not as bad as he believes. It may be that there is an afterlife after all (who really knows?), and it may be that science and progress can make the world a happier place (though these days the prospects do not look so good).

The interesting thing, though, is that his system really ends on a happy note. He *does* have confidence that evolution will finally succeed in its end and all suffering will ultimately cease. So in the last analysis is he really a pessimist or an optimist?

9

The Zen of Life and Death

"You know," added Tweedledee very gravely, "it's one of the most serious things that can possibly happen to one in a battle—to get one's head cut off."

Alice laughed loud: But she managed to turn it into a cough, for fear of hurting his feelings.

Lewis Carroll, *Through the Looking Glass*, Chapter 4

The subject of life and death appears to be of some general interest, and so a discussion of this topic may not be out of order. The only trouble is that just about anything one can say on this subject is probably wrong!

The Zen master Huang Po said about the mind, "Begin to reason about it, and you at once fall into error." I think that the same can be said even more aptly about life and death. All discussions of this subject somehow tend to miss the mark. Then why discuss it? I could give a Zen-like answer and say, "Why not?" The fact is that we *are* interested in these things and to repress these interests is kind of silly. Of course, many regard such discussions as essentially morbid. This is beautifully illustrated by Bertrand Russell's story of the man at a banquet who was asked what he thought would happen to him after his death. He seemed very uneasy and tried to avoid the question. But the questioner persisted and finally the man said, "I suppose I shall enter paradise and enjoy total bliss for all eternity, but must we talk about such unpleasant subjects?"

A somewhat related incident is the following. Once we had a dinner party. I jokingly said about one of the guests (a very close friend of mine), "Don't give him too much to drink; he gets hostile and belligerent." His wife then said, "He goes through several stages, one of which is that he becomes infuriated with the idea that one day he will have to die." My friend is only in his late twenties. Another guest, a gentleman in his early sixties, turned to him and said, "Are you not a bit young to be worrying about that? Do you really find life that wonderful?" My friend replied, "Oh, yes." He then went on to describe how he simply could not conceive of himself as not existing, the idea of which was infinitely frightening and repugnant. He then added, "I would be less disturbed by the thought of being eternally in hell than of not existing at all." I told my friend that I found it rather odd and puzzling that he should find nonexistence both inconceivable *and* frightening. Either one alone I could understand perfectly, but how could something be both nonunderstandable and frightening? The very fact that he could have such a positive emotional reaction as fear attached to a given notion would indicate that he had to have *some* idea of the notion. He admitted that this was indeed puzzling but found no reassurance in these considerations. I then suggested that what perhaps disturbed him was the thought that time should somehow continue without him, and I asked him, "Would it disturb you as much if tomorrow time itself would suddenly stop, so there never would come an actual time when you were dead?" He replied that the question was meaningless to him since he could form absolutely no notion at all of what it could mean for time itself to stop. I can't blame him too much for his reaction though I do not find the idea of time stopping so unconceivable. At any rate, I pressed this particular point no further although I did partake of the very lively discussion about life and death that persisted most of the evening.

The next day, my young friend and I reviewed some of the events of the previous evening. He told me with a mischievous smile that at parties, he would always bring up the subject of death and that the conversation would then remain on this subject all night, sometimes without his saying any more. What particularly impressed him was everybody's desperate attempts to convince him that there was really nothing for him to worry about! But he believed that the very urgency of their attempts indicated their own desperation at the thought that there really *was* something to worry about. I think that there is much truth in this observation. Since we all do have certain unresolved inner desperations about the matter, I think it helpful that we all *do* think about and discuss these matters as freely as possible. *Is* there really something to worry about? I believe not. But many will interpret this as a sort of wishful thinking, or "whistling in the dark." I will return to this question later.

One can approach the question of life and death in many ways. One is from the viewpoint of authority and revelation. Another is from the viewpoint of science and reason, that is, to consider all evidence for and against survival and then balance their probabilities and then decide which is the more "likely." Related to this approach is the analytic one: First determine whether the expression, "I can survive my bodily death," has any meaning at all before deciding whether it is true or false. Another somewhat related approach is to consider various meanings of the word *survive*. Then one can take the psychological approach by considering what are the psychological motivations behind one's attitudes toward the matter and to investigate how much of one's beliefs in survival or nonsurvival is simply the result of wishful thinking.

I believe that all these approaches are weak but shall consider some aspects of them, perhaps mainly to give the reader my feeling for their essential futility. Then I shall consider some mystical and

Eastern approaches to the question. These approaches strike me as not wholly satisfactory but nevertheless better than any others I know.

Authority and Revelation

Here I face a bit of a quandary. On the one hand, I never have had very much confidence in revelation and still less in authority. (As I once said to a friend, "Why should I believe in other people's revelations? I have enough trouble believing my own.") Yet my final attitude may come closer to revelation than anything else. That is about as much as I can say about this at the moment.

Analysis, Science, and Types of Survival

In the so-called analytic approach, one often examines a statement in terms of what it means before deciding whether or not it is true. Take, for example, the statement, "I will survive my bodily death." Some claim that the statement is true, others that it is false, others that it is certainly either true or false but we don't know which, others that it has no meaning whatsoever, and still others that if it has any meaning they don't know what the meaning could be. For example, the logical positivist Moritz Schlick regarded this proposition as perfectly meaningful and *possibly* true. As he said, "I can perfectly well imagine being present at and witnessing my own funeral." On the other hand, the logical positivist A. J. Ayer believed Schlick's statement to be not merely false but self-contradictory. (That's a rather drastic difference of opinion, isn't it?) Other logical positivists claim the proposition to be neither true nor false nor self-contradictory but simply meaningless. Since they claim not to understand what this self, soul, spirit, mind, or psyche is apart from the body, then they do not know just what it is that is said to survive or not to survive. Of course, a pure materialist might define the mind to be simply a person's memories and behavioral dispositions.[1] To such a materialist, one possible meaning of survival (and indeed the only one I can think of) is that at some future time after one's death another physical organism would be in the universe with the same memories and behavioral dispositions (a sort of resurrection). Such a materialist would most likely concede the logical possibility of this type of survival but would hold it as fantastically improbable. At any rate, surely this is *not* what Schlick meant! Otherwise, we would have the funny picture of another man at Schlick's funeral with the same memories, dispositions, and very personality of Schlick looking at the corpse of the old Schlick. (At least I find this situation funny, don't you?) No, this "physicalistic" type of survival, though of possible interest, is definitely beyond the scope of this enquiry. I am interested in discussing what might be called *psychic survival*, that is, the survival of the soul, psyche, or self.

What kind of survival do I have in mind? Actually, there is more than one notion of survival, and we should take a look at some of them. First, there is of course the Christian notion of the soul's surviving with all its memories and personal characteristics. Some Christians think of this survival in terms of bodily resurrection, others in the more Platonic terms of the soul leaving its body and entering a purely spiritual realm. The distinction between these two notions is not too significant for our present purposes; both are certainly concerned with individual or personal survival. Next we consider reincarnation. According to this notion, the spirit of the departed enters the body of a new living organism—human, animal, or possibly even plant—but *without* its memories. Many people who have a perfect understanding (though not necessarily belief) in the Christian notion of survival with one's memories find this Eastern notion of reincarnation—survival *without memories*—simply inconceivable! What on earth, they ask, could the self be without its memories and own individual characteristics? I myself don't have the *slightest* difficulty with this notion. I have a most definite concept of what I mean by *I*, and my memories and particular personal characteristics seem to me to be no more part of this essential *I* than the clothes I wear! If the reader asks me what then *do* I mean by *I*, I'm afraid that I can no more tell him than I can describe my sensation of red to a blind man. If the reader wishes to conclude from this that I only deceive myself in thinking that I have such a notion, that such a notion is really meaningless, of course he is free to. I think, however, that he should bear in mind that the inability to define a given notion in terms of a set of other "known" notions is not necessarily indicative of the meaninglessness of that notion; it may in principle simply not be so definable. I recall that someone once said to me, "After all, when you die, various babies will be born. How do you know one of them won't be you?" Several persons present simply could not understand what he was saying. I think that I understood perfectly! Of course, one of them *could* be me; the question is, *Will* one of them be me?

How attractive is this notion of reincarnation compared with, say, the Christian notion of survival with one's memories? This, of course, is a matter of individual taste. Personally, I find the idea of reincarnation extremely attractive. The idea of cyclic rebirth has a wonderful, sparkling freshness that appeals to me even more than the idea of continuing, as it were, on a straight line, which seems rather stale and tiresome. But this, of course, does not mean that I necessarily *believe* it. There is all the difference in the world between finding an idea attractive and believing it is necessarily true. This is beautifully brought out in the following passage of Suzuki on transmigration (reincarnation):

> I do not know whether transmigration can be proved or maintained on the scientific level, but I know that it is an inspiring theory and full of poetic suggestions, and I am satisfied with this interpretation and do not seem to have any desire to go beyond it. To me, the idea of transmigration has a personal appeal, and as to its scientific and philosophical implications, I leave it to the study of the reader.[2]

There is a curious variant of reincarnation that I wish to mention briefly. According to this variant, the soul is not a simple, indecomposable substance but a composite that after death simply gets recycled (just like the material of our bodies gets recycled). After death, instead of my entering the body of just one newborn baby (or other organism), I would split up into a multitude of them. If there is one thing I cannot imagine, it is the thought of my splitting up! (Even total annihilation is easier for me to comprehend than that!) Perhaps, though, I should modify this statement in light of the following past experience.

I am not sure whether it was during a dream or a hypnagogic reverie; I rather believe it was the latter. At any rate, I experienced myself as dead and turning into a cluster of bacteria—fresh, live bacteria! It was not as if I were detatchedly watching my *body* turn into bacteria; it was *I* who was turning into them and gaining my very life *through* them. Also—and this is most important—I did not at all feel as if I were a *victim,* as if the bacteria were preying upon me, sacrificing me for their own ends. *I* was the principal gainer of the transaction. Indeed, it was not quite clear to me where I left off and the bacteria began; the bacteria were *me!* Thus, I should have more understanding for the recycling hypothesis. The only difference is that I did not think of the bacteria as *individuals;* I did not have any sense that I was splitting up into these individuals. Rather, I thought of this bacterial cluster as a whole unit, and I was simply becoming this unit.

Next I wish to consider the so-called scientific arguments against the probability of survival. Frankly, these seem to me incredibly poor! What I now have to say is, of course, only pertinent to dualists, who think of mind and matter as distinct substances and who know perfectly well what it means for the soul to survive but who have grave doubts that in fact it will. I am thinking of one dualist who argued thus: In principle, it is conceivable that the soul survives, but in the light of scientific evidence, it is extremely improbable. Since the parallelism between psychical and physical events during our lifetime is so clearly in evidence, then scientific induction requires us to believe that the parallelism should continue after our death.

There are two aspects of this point of view that I wish to dispute. The first is this: Does scientific induction really require it? Suppose, for example, that a certain reaction between two chemicals is always observed provided that they are mixed in a platinum container. Scientific induction does indeed require us to predict that the same reaction will occur if they are again mixed in a platinum container but does not allow us to predict what will happen if they are mixed outside such a container. Similarly, the fact that a parallelism exists between psychic and physical events and that this parallelism exists during one's lifetime does not warrant the belief that it should probably continue to exist after one's lifetime.

I have a second objection, perhaps more serious yet. Suppose it be granted that the parallelism does continue to hold after death. Does this imply the annihilation of the psyche? It seems to me that it does not! After all, when the body dies, it does not just disappear. It gets eventually transformed (in all likelihood) to other living beings like bacteria, worms, and so forth, which in turn are transformed into the bodies of higher living mammals. Strangely, the dualist who disbelieves in the survival of the soul nevertheless believes that the body still exists after death. This certainly does not seem like a continuing parallelism but rather a drastic bifurcation: The body continues to exist, but the soul gets annihilated! In this regard, it is curious that one speaks of dead bodies but never of dead souls, except in the form of ghosts or sometimes departed souls. But a departed soul seems to mean something very different from a dead soul. The former is a soul that has gone elsewhere; the latter, one that no more goes elsewhere than a dead body goes elsewhere but rather somehow changes its state. I must confess that I hardly know what I mean by a dead soul, but if the parallelism between mind and matter should persist after death, then just as the body dies but does not go out of existence, the soul should also die but not go out of existence. If the body (or perhaps rather the material of the body) comes to life again in the form of other living organisms, then similarly the corresponding soul substance should come to life. So if anything, it would seem that if scientific induction requires us to project into the future an assumed parallelism between body and mind, then this should add support to something like reincarnation rather than annihilation. But as I said before, I do not believe that sound scientific methodology does require us to make this projection. Goodness gracious, if I have a remarkably consistent dream in which I observe a high correlation between certain experiences and others, what rational grounds exist for my expecting this correlation to continue after I wake up? To put the matter another way, it is not at all inconceivable to me that one day scientific technology will enable us to anesthetize the body of a subject and then connect a mass of electrodes directly to his brain and nerve centers, thus inducing a whole artificial life or sort of "dream world." (This idea is, of course, quite common in science fiction.) So if, for instance, the correct visual and tactile nerve centers are stimulated, the subject will have as vivid an experience of a material object as we have of objects in the (so-called) real world. Now, in this artificially induced life, the subject might also experience a "body" that he thinks is his own. He will observe a perfect correlation between his own perceptions and feelings with events that he observes taking place in his "body." Let us also assume that his "dream" is programmed to last, say, ten years. As part of his "dream," he observes other bodies, like the body that he calls his own, dying. Also let us assume that all memories prior to his "dream" have been obliterated; his "dream world" is the only world he knows. My point now is that under these conditions the subject would have the same grounds as we have for believing that upon the death of his "body" he would go out of existence, but of course he would be wrong. Furthermore, I have no reason to believe that this situation is not right now happening to me! I don't for a moment believe that it is, but I have no rational evidence that it is not. Some may say that it is highly improbable that I am now in the state of this subject. But I do not see any way of evaluating the probability of such an event, and what experiments could I possibly perform to throw any light on its probability? What experiments could a dreamer possibly perform in his dream to evaluate the probability of his dreaming? It seems to me none whatsoever! Thus I believe: (1) It is logically possible that I am in this state; (2) as a matter of fact, I am not in this state; (3) I have no evidence for this belief, but I believe it anyhow; and (4) probability has absolutely nothing to do with the matter. And so I believe about the question of survival after death: (1) that there is not the slightest rational or probabilist evidence that one survives; and (2) that there is not the slightest rational or probabilist evidence that one doesn't.

Wishful Thinking?

Now let us consider the psychological approach to the motivations of beliefs about survival from the point of view of how much of our beliefs concerning these matters are merely the result of wishful thinking. The unfortunate aspect of this approach—or rather about many of those who take it—is that they seem to regard the statement, "That's only wishful thinking," as a valid counterargument. I'm sure most of my readers are too sophisticated for that, but it is surprising how many people are not! At any rate, this approach is curiously one-sided when applied to the subject of life and death. The usual argument, of course, is, "First there is no evidence for the existence of the soul. Secondly, even if there is a soul, there is absolutely no evidence for its survival after death, and plenty of evidence against it. Yet many otherwise intelligent people in fact do believe in survival. Why is this? The only sensible explanation is that —whether they consciously know it or not—their desire for immortality is so intense, that it totally warps their objectivity about the matter."[3] Now, to those who dismiss belief in survival as mere wishful thinking, I would like to ask the following questions: What would you say about those who claim not to care whether or not they survive, or even express preference for nonsurvival, but who nevertheless strongly believe that they will survive? Would you say that really deep down they *do* want to survive and that they are only fooling themselves in thinking that they don't? What about those who believe in hell and that they are utterly evil and are frightened to death of their impending damnation, and who say, "I wish that we *didn't* survive, but the horrible thing is that we do!" I guess you would say that even the thought of hell terrifies them less than the thought of extinction, so it still is a matter of wishful thinking even though superficially it seems like fearful thinking. (As some Freudians say, fears are often disguised wishes.) What about those Eastern philosophers who believe in reincarnation but regard it as a curse rather than a blessing. All their endeavors are geared toward *avoiding* rebirth, and they believe and hope that with sufficient effort and insight rebirth can be avoided. Perhaps you would again say that deep down even the Easterner desires some form of survival but really knows that he cannot have it and so turns to the remarkable extreme of not merely saying that rebirth is undesirable (which is merely a sour grapes attitude) but makes it his most profound life purpose to try to prevent the very thing that he (unconsciously) most desires! Of course, one can also attack the Easterner for his wishful thinking along very different lines, but I imagine this line of attack would occur to relatively few Westerners. What I have in mind is this: Imagine someone brought up in the East who has absorbed the attitude that existence is suffering and has absolutely no doubts about rebirth, but who is a total skeptic concerning the possibility of avoiding it. He might well say, "We all know damn well that none of us wants to be reborn, and we all know—deep down—that we must be. So this Buddhistic and Hindoo talk that it is possible to avoid rebirth is sheer wishful thinking!"

A somewhat amusing incident comes to mind. I was once telling a friend (a gifted mathematician) that the hypothesis of survival seemed to me perfectly plausible. His immediate reaction (like that of Ayer) was that the idea was totally meaningless. But later in the conversation, he insisted that my belief in the possibility of survival resulted purely from the fact that I *wanted* to survive. Several years later, we met again, and I reminded him of the conversation. I said, "One thing puzzles me. I can understand what you mean when you say that my views on survival reflect wishful thinking. And I can understand—at least in part—when you say that my notion of survival is *meaningless*. But I cannot understand what you can mean when you put the two together. If, as you say, I wish to survive, then I must be wishing for *something*. Hence, I fail to see how that which I wish for—which I call *survival*—can be an empty notion. I can't see how I can wish for nothing." He replied, "I thought of that, and I was a little hard on you." I then pointed out that it was not that he was hard on *me* but that there was a purely logical difficulty to be straightened out: How can I wish for x when x is not merely nonexistent but *meaningless*? He replied, "What I really should have said is that what you are really wishing for is that your *body* live forever, and since you know that is impossible, then you have invented this notion of soul, and, as a substitute, hope that *it* will survive." I must confess that I am still puzzled! If I really have invented this notion of soul (or more realistically, if I have borrowed this notion from others who have invented it), then I have also invented the notion of the survival of the soul. I therefore have attached *some* meaning to the term, so how can it be meaningless?

If one must persist in using the ad hominem argument of wishful thinking, then I can think of another target that, it seems to me, has not yet been sufficiently or widely attacked. I am thinking of people like, for instance, Bertrand Russell, who reject survival as highly improbable but still maintain that there is nothing to worry about. They then proceed to give a whole host of reasons why survival is not even desirable and to explain the benefits that will accrue if individuals *don't* survive. These people pride themselves on their lack of wishful thinking. But it seems to me that their attitude can just as much be interpreted as a sour grapes attitude: "Who wants to survive, anyhow?" Of course, they are free from the (wishful) thought that they do survive, but the belief that they don't *want* to survive may be wishful thinking. I would like to put the matter another way. The groups to whom I refer evidently take the attitude, "It is only wishful thinking to believe that we survive. But we can be perfectly happy and content with the universe without this childish belief that we survive." My question now is, "Is it not possible that it is only wishful thinking to believe that we can be content without the belief in survival?" In a way, one might admire some of the existentialists who see this, and whose attitudes might be paraphrased, "Of course we don't survive, and of course we want to survive, so let's stop kidding ourselves that we don't want to survive. Instead, let us squarely face the infinitely painful fact that we do want to survive, but we can't. This is the true tragedy of life." To the great annoyance of many—and at the risk of being accused of rationalizing—I must nevertheless raise the question whether *this* attitude may not also be a form of wishful thinking, though perhaps of a somewhat different sort. Is there perhaps not such a thing as *masochistic* or *sadistic* wishful thinking? Is there not such a thing as *pessimistic* wishful thinking just as well as the (perhaps) more usual *optimistic* wishful thinking? For people who take a delight in how *bad* things are, is it so inappropriate to suspect them of wishful thinking when they exaggerate the bad aspects of life so ridiculously? While we are at it, is it not possible that *all* forms of thought are wishful thinking? Who knows, maybe one day some psychologist will prove that the real reason I believe in the laws of logic and mathematics is that I want to. At least, I cannot prove that some psychologist will not prove this.

At this point, things are getting a little ridiculous, aren't they? I think that the upshot of all this is that to be overly concerned about whether one's beliefs are or are not the result of wishful thinking is very bad, ultimately destroying, rather than aiding, the objectivity of one's judgment. Not only that, but this concern may well prevent one from knowing what he really thinks. How many fine thoughts have been repressed because it is feared that they may be only wishful thinking? This consideration is not unrelated to our next topic, for which I will coin the phrase *fearful thinking.*

I understand *wishful thinking* to be that thinking based on wish rather than evidence. Similarly, I would define *fearful thinking* as that thinking likewise not based on evidence but based purely on fear. Both wishful thinking and fearful thinking are equally lacking in objectivity.

Why would one engage in fearful thinking? I have already suggested masochism as one explanation. But another explanation may be more pertinent. I think tht one tends to believe that the worst will happen so as not to build up false hopes and thus be disappointed. So, for example, those who hysterically and fanatically insist that there is no afterlife are terrified lest they expect something good that in fact may not come to pass. Their fear, so to speak, is that they may live in a fool's paradise. Fearful thinking may be described as bending over backward to avoid wishful thinking. But I must again emphasize that it is just as open as wishful thinking to subjective error. To put the matter another way, I would say that just as those who insist that there is an afterlife may be engaged in purely wishful thinking, those who insist that there isn't are just as subjectively biased, only in the direction of fearful thinking.

Now let us forget about wishful and fearful thinking and ask ourselves honestly why we *are* in fact so disturbed by the thought of death. Many readers will reply, "*You* may be so disturbed, but *I* am not!" But I honestly find this rather doubtful. I believe that a few exceptional people are genuinely not disturbed but that many others only tend to repress their disturbance. After all, so many social factors encourage us to deny—even to ourselves—any fear of death. We are encouraged to "banish any such gloomy thoughts from our minds and to dwell on the beautiful things of life and on those lives to come." We are taught that fears of our own death are unmanly, cowardly, selfish, "egocentric," and so forth. One well-known writer said something to the effect that the charge of selfishness concerning our distress about death is unfair; it's not that we are worried about ourselves, we are worried about our loved ones, and we cannot bear the thought that they should perish. Although I *do* believe that we are also concerned about our loved ones, I find it a bit sad that people should be so worried about their selfishness. Of course we are very much worried about ourselves, and why shouldn't we be? All these moralistic charges of selfishness, cowardice, and so forth leave me quite unimpressed.

I now want to turn to an analysis of why we are in fact disturbed by the thought of *our* dying. My purpose is not to reassure the reader who is disturbed that there is nothing to worry about but rather to take a look at what in fact is really worrying him. The first thing that of course leaps to mind is the thought of those who *do* enjoy life: "What a pity it must end! Just think of all the good things I will miss." Then there is the rather deeper and more terrifying feeling that death is a state of loneliness, darkness, isolation, or separation from the rest of the world. It does little good to point out that it is really meaningless to talk of separation between something nonexistent and something existent, for we still have the psychological *association* of separateness. But the very feeling that after death we are separated from the rest of the world only indicates that we do think of ourselves as somehow existing after our death! Indeed, it is literally inconceivable to us that we can ever cease to exist. Here, I think, lies the true heart of the trouble! I believe it is not so much *fear* that is troubling us. The real trouble lies in our *trying to force ourselves to believe something that in fact is psychologically incapable of being believed!* One of Goethe's arguments for immortality is that a person cannot even conceive of his nonexistence; how then can he possibly believe it? This argument strikes me as quite remarkable. Not that I draw from it the conclusion that we *are* immortal, but I believe that Goethe came closest of all to the real reason why people do believe in immortality. This factor seems to be far stronger than the motive of wishful thinking. How can we conceivably believe in our nonexistence? Yet there are very powerful social pressures to make us feel that we should (e.g., considerations of trying to be rational, avoidance of wishful thinking, etc.). So I believe that *fear* of death is not the real issue; the real issue is the conflict between our deepest intuitions and the social pressures exerted on us to deny them. Stated otherwise, I grant that many of us are indeed disturbed by the thought of our dying, but I believe that our disturbance is not really fear—as it appears to be—but rather the result of our trying to force ourselves to believe that which we are not capable of believing.

Personal Views

In this section, I shall state some purely personal views on the subject of life and death. I have already considered this subject from several angles—analytic, scientific, and psychological. I believe that a certain degree of objectivity in these matters is of great value, but I don't believe that we should therefore neglect a purely subjective approach or that such an approach is worthless. After all, we do have our own intuitions in addition to our reasoning powers, and why should we allow either to be subservient to the other?

When I talk of taking a purely subjective approach, what I have in mind is to simply state what one really does believe without worrying about whether the belief is or is not rational or whether it is or is not the result of some form of wishful thinking. This is less easy than may be imagined. Even if we temporarily waive all requirements of justifying our beliefs, it is not all that easy to know just what our beliefs really are. At least I find it so—particularly about such topics as life and death.

Suppose I now honestly ask myself what I believe will really happen to me after my bodily death; will I continue to exist or will I go out of existence? To tell the absolute truth, both answers seem to me somehow wrong! The idea of going out of existence or of ceasing to exist is to me absolutely inconceivable, hence I (in the good company of Goethe) cannot possibly believe something that I cannot even understand—something that I can form no notion of. Therefore, I am forced to rule out the possibility of my ceasing to exist. From this, it might appear to follow that I believe I will continue to exist after my bodily death. But this is not so. I am open to the possibility that I will, but I have no particular reason to believe that I necessarily will. What about the proposition, "Either I will continue existing, or I will cease to exist." Do I believe that? My answer is emphatically, "NO!" Now, this might appear to be completely contrary to the normally accepted Aristotelian logic with its classical principle of the excluded middle.[4] If it does, I would not feel too bad, for although I fully accept classical logic in the exact sciences, I have some doubts that it is fruitful in the present area. But I don't believe that my drastic rejection of this (apparent) disjunction really does violate the law of the excluded middle. Its truth is really dependent on (at least) three tacit premises: (1) The word *I* really denotes something; (2) there really is such a thing as time; and (3) I am in time.

As to (1), we shall discuss this further in the next section. As to (2), the denial of the reality of time goes counter to common sense but is nevertheless a cardinal point believed—or rather felt—by many mystics. Suppose a mystic is asked, "Are you really serious about denying the reality of time? You really do not believe that some events occur before others?" Such a mystic—if he has a modicum of some philosophical orientation—might answer something like, "Of course, events occur in the phenomenal world—the world of appearance—and hence time may be said to exist in the world of appearance. But time does not exist in the world of reality." I do not wish to now go into this highly interesting question; for purposes of this essay let me grant that time really exists. But this still leaves open the question whether I am really in time.

If it surprises you that I have some doubts that I am really in time, let me say that it is of course obvious that I experience time, and I experience events in the normal time sequence. But does this necessarily mean that I—the experiencer—have to be in time for this to happen? Why can't I be outside time and experience moments of time nevertheless? Am I something that actually moves through time; or am I stationary, with time moving past me?

I realize that at this point I am becoming what the logical positivists would call ridiculously metaphysical, making one pseudostatement after another and asking one pseudoquestion after another. I hope that those of you who are positivistically oriented will at least give me credit for knowing what I am doing in the sense of realizing perfectly that the questions I am discussing *are not questions about the physical world* and are hence totally outside the scope of science. Therefore, scientific methods cannot be of help in this discussion, so if one wants to stick wholly to logic and the methods of the physical sciences, one will have to turn to a different topic.

To return to the topic of time, as I said, it is not at all certain to me that because I experience time I am necessarily in time. If I am not in time, then the entire question of whether I will survive my bodily death becomes meaningless—the question simply disappears!

But am I really outside time, or is my thought that I am only another example of wishful thinking? To tell you the truth, I don't know that either! To say that I am outside time does not strike me as quite right. To say that I am in time does not strike me as wholly right either. Is it necessarily true that I am either in time or outside time? I doubt that also!

Let me put it this way: I normally believe that I am inside time, but when I reflect on the matter, I am no longer so sure of this. Although it is wrong to conclude from the above that I am *outside* time, for my purposes it is enough that I do not believe that I am inside time; I therefore do not have to believe either that I will survive my bodily death or I won't!

I feel the same way, incidentally, about the question of my existence prior to my bodily birth. Did I really begin in the year 1919? I doubt that very much! Did I exist before 1919? I doubt that also. (This reminds me somewhat of the Kantian antinomy of whether the universe had a beginning or not.)[5]

This about sums up my real feelings about life and death. Do I really believe I am not in time? Not wholly and not constantly; sometimes I do and sometimes I don't. (Doesn't this sound silly: Some*times* I believe I am in time and some*times* I don't? But it becomes less silly when one distinguishes experiencing time from being in time.)

Some people might say that they can form absolutely no notion of what it could possibly mean not to be in time. I would like to ask them the following question: Can you conceive the possibility of there being more than one time series (as in some science fiction stories)? If so, can you imagine being in a different one than this one? Assuming there were more than one time series, what would immortality mean? Would it necessarily mean continuing forever in *this* one? If you believe that upon your bodily death, you would no longer be in this time series but would jump into another one, would that satisfy you? Perhaps you could conceive of there being many different time series and of your being in *any* one of them but not of being in *none* of them!

I am afraid that the whole problem of survival is intimately bound up with our very notions of time, which—except for purposes of science and practical, everyday living—are none too satisfactory. As I said at the beginning of this essay, I suspect that *all* thinking about these questions is somehow off the track, and I certainly don't except my own. My hunch is that those who believe in immortality are closer to the truth than those who do not but still miss the real point. It is possible that the entire question is still not adequately formulated. To this topic I now turn.

Some Eastern Approaches

When I say that the whole question of life and death may be inadequately formulated, I am thinking of the Buddhist notion that the *I* is simply a fiction, despite our usual intuitions to the contrary. If this is true, then the whole notion of survival takes on a totally different significance. Buddhist thought regards psychic reality as a stream of consciousness that has no *agent*. (This position is like that of David Hume, who did not believe in the existence of the so-called self.) If this is so, then fear of death—or the feeling that death is a tragedy—is really ludicrous. It would be like a group of people who are worried that a certain town is going to be bombed; The optimists say, "No, it won't be bombed, it will survive." The pessimists say, "That is only wishful thinking; the town will be destroyed." And then it turns out that the town they are all arguing about doesn't even exist!

Personally, I am somewhat dubious about Buddhist metaphysics. I find far more comprehensible the Brahmanic, or orthodox Hindu, notion that the *I* is not a fiction but is nevertheless quite different from what we think. It may be that the individual *I* does not exist, but the universal *I* does. Rather, it may be that what we think is the individual *I* is in reality the universal *I*. (My God, if the *universal I* disappeared upon the death of just one individual, then there *would* be something to worry about! It would mean that *nothing* would be left! I would not be surprised if deep down *that* is what we are really worried about!)

Again, it may be misleading to talk of the individual *I* and the universal *I*; perhaps we should talk of only one *I*. This seems to me the most important idea in Brahmanic philosophy. Let me elaborate a little.

Obviously, I make a distinction between your sensations, feelings, and thoughts and mine. But from this it does not follow that the agent who experiences your thoughts is different from the agent who experiences mine. The question is, Are the agents really the same? It may seem completely counterintuitive that they are. But this intuition really appears to be culturally induced. It seems that the intuition of most Westerners is, "Of course they are not the same. I am I, and you are you, and that's all there is to it." But the intuition of many Easterners really seems to be that you and I are literally the same person.

Is not this the central issue of Brahmanism? It strikes me as far more radical and thoroughgoing than the Hegelian and post-Hegelian ideas of the Absolute, which is something like an "over-soul" that, so to speak, *includes* your soul and mine but is somehow infinitely greater than both. By contrast, the Brahmanic idea is far more drastic. Indeed, it appears to come close to outraging logic itself. It is that you and I are not *parts* of some supreme being but that we are the *very same being.*

I hope that you realize the fantastic ramifications that this hypothesis has on the question of life and death! Assume for the moment that the hypothesis is true. It follows that I will *not* die upon my bodily death as long as one other live creature remains, for this creature is also me. I hence do not have to believe in my soul going to a spiritual realm or in reincarnation. I already *am* reincarnated; rather, I am already incarnated in all other conscious beings. So when my body dies, there will be countless copies of *me* left. Indeed, whether your body dies or my body dies, the effect will be no different on me (or on you, which is the same thing).

Is it not possible that all of us deep down feel that this idea has some truth in it and that's why we in fact don't fear death more than we do? Is it not possible that this is the real reason we treat each other as well as we do, and why we are as concerned as we are about protecting each other's lives? It is our *own* lives we are protecting!

In many ways, this viewpoint is quite remarkable! To use another analogy—an elaboration of one devised by Schopenhauer—imagine looking at a point of light through a crystal. We see a thousand images, but they are all of the very same point. Similarly, our individual selves are but multiple appearances of one fundamental self. An individual death, then, is like blocking off a single facet of the crystal, and an individual birth is like opening up another facet. So the images vary and change and come and go, dancing their "dance of life," but the real point of light remains totally unaltered during the whole procedure.

A similar analogy is drawn by the Vedanta. It likens the relation of the one true self and its individual selves to the one sun simultaneously illuminating a thousand rooms of a palace. The rooms are of course like the individuals. Each has its own individual light but not its individual source of light. Thus (this is *my* analogy), an individual death is like drawing a shade or curtain on the window of an individual room. The individual room, it is true, goes dark. But none of the sunlight is lost! Not even that portion of light that formerly illuminated the room is lost; it now illuminates the shade or curtain. If the pedantic reader asks, "But suppose the shade or curtain is dark brown or black?" my answer is, "Yes, then the *light* gets lost, but not the energy of the light, which is transformed into heat."

Some Chinese Thoughts on the Subject

Having touched a little on the Buddhist and Brahmanic approaches, I would like to conclude with some contributions made by Chinese philosophy to the subject.

When Confucius was asked to expostulate on the nature of death, he replied that we do not even know the nature of Life; how then can we talk of the nature of Death?"

Confucius's reply strikes me as quite sound albeit a trifle pedestrian. My favorite writers of all (on this as well as many other matters) are the Taoists such as Laotse, Liehtse, and Chuangtse. They give neither analogies nor any rational explanations whatsoever! In total defiance of all logic, they soar their merry way upward like birds in free flight.

For example, Laotse once said that he who dies but does not perish has life everlasting.

It is amazing how differently people react to this! Some (like myself) simply burst out laughing. Others become very solemn and serious and try to analyze what distinction Laotse could possibly have had in mind between dying and perishing. But I can assure you that any such analysis will totally miss the point! The line means absolutely neither more nor less than exactly what it says.

I love the incident from Liehtse about the group who came across a skull. Many of the group recoiled in horror. But one member said, "Both the skull and I know that there is no such absolute thing as life and death."

Finally, there is the following gorgeous passage from Chuangtse —one of the most remarkable passages ever written.[6]

> Nan-po asked Nu-yu, "Sir, you are old, but have the look of a child. How is this?"
>
> "I have learned Tao," replied Nu-yu.
>
> "Can Tao be learned?" Nan-po said.
>
> "Ah! How can it?" replied Nu-yu.
>
> "You are not the type of man. Pu-liang—I had the ability of the sage but did not know the teachings. I knew all the teachings but did not have his ability. But still I had to teach him. It was three days before he was able to transcend this world. After he transcended this world, I waited for seven days more and then he was able to transcend all material things. After he transcended all material things, I waited for nine days more and then he was able to transcend all life. Having transcended all life, he became as clear and bright as the morning. Having become as clear and bright as the morning, he was able to see the One. Having seen the One, he was then able to abolish the distinction of past and present. Having abolished the past and present, he was then able to enter the realm of neither life nor death. . . .

Where else does one find a passage this wonderful? Apart from the marvelous phrase, "he became as clear and bright as the morning," there is the more immediately relevant phrase, "the realm of neither life nor death."

The concept of the realm of neither life nor death comes closer to what I have tried to say in this essay than anything I have been able to say. It is a perfect example of why I so love Chinese philosophy!

I can think of no better conclusion to this essay than to quote a passage of the Chinese Zen master Huang Po (T'ang dynasty). Of it, the translator John Blofield says, "This paragraph is, perhaps, one of the finest expositions of Zen teaching, for it encompasses in a few words almost the entire scope of that vast and penetrating wisdom."[7]

If an ordinary man, when he is about to die, could only see the five elements of consciousness as void; the four physical elements as not constituting an "I"; the real Mind as formless and neither coming nor going; his nature as something neither commencing at his birth nor perishing at his death, but as whole and motionless in its very depths; his Mind and environmental objects as one—if he could really accomplish this, he would receive Enlightenment in a flash. He would no longer be entangled by the Triple World; he would be a World-Transcendor. He would be without even the faintest tendency toward rebirth. If he should behold the glorious sight of all the Buddhas coming to welcome him, surrounded by every kind of gorgeous manifestation, he would feel no desire to approach them. If he should behold all sorts of horrific forms surrounding him, he would experience no terror. He would just be himself, oblivious of conceptual thought and one with the Absolute. He would have attained the state of unconditioned being. This, then, is the fundamental principle.[8]

Notes

1. See the viewpoint of the realistic mystic in Chapter 5, "Simplicus and the Tree."

2. Daisetz Suzuki, *Mysticism: Christian and Buddhist* in *World Perspectives*, Vol. 12, edited by Ruth Anshen (New York: Harper and Brothers, 1957), p. 126.

3. On the whole I admire Dean Inge's statement (William R. Inge, *Christian Mysticism* (London: Methuen & Co., 1912, p. 55n.): "The allegation that the Christian persuades himself of a future life because it is the most comfortable belief to hold, seems to be utterly contemptible. Certain views about heaven and hell are no doubt traceable to shallow optimism; but the belief in immortality is in itself rather awful than consoling. Besides, what sane man would wish to be deceived in such a matter?" Much as I admire this statement as a whole, there are three small points that disturb me somewhat. First, I wish Dean Inge had used a less harsh word

than *contemptible.* Second, I find it surprising that he should regard immortality as somewhat "awful." And third, I feel that his comment, "Certain views about heaven and hell are no doubt traceable to shallow optimism," warrants the same criticism that he is leveling at those who dismiss belief in survival as traceable to mere optimism.

4. This principle is that every proposition is either true or false.

5. If it did, then there must have been a time before the beginning. If it didn't, then an infinite past has come to an end, which (according to Kant) is also impossible.

6. *A Source Book in Chinese Philosophy,* translated and compiled by Wing-Tsit Chan (Princeton: Princeton University Press, 1963), p. 195.

7. John Blofield, trans., *The Zen Teachings of Huang Po* (New York: Grove Press, 1958), pp. 45–46.

8. Ibid.

10

What Is There?

This chapter is a bit technical. The reader who finds it too difficult can skip it without loss of continuity.

Ontology

One dictionary defines *ontology* as the science of being; the branch of metaphysics that investigates the nature of being and of the essence of things.

This sounds like a rather ambitious subject, don't you think? I am reminded of the following passage from *Sherlock Holmes in Tibet* by Richard Wincor.[1] Holmes is speaking.

On the 15th September 1891, the Vice-Chancellor advised me that I was to be one of several qualified Westerners to attend a special session conducted by Tibet's leading metaphysician, Lama Nordup. The session was scheduled in a fortnight's time; all of us were to clear out of Tibet a day later. Somewhat puzzled, I asked the Vice-Chancellor what the lama's subject would be. His reply (translated literally in these notes) was,

"The secret of life and death, and the mysteries of existence."
This reply captured my interest somewhat, and I resolved to
attend.

Quine starts his famous essay *On What There Is* with the words,
"A curious thing about the ontological problems is its simplicity. It
can be put in three Anglo-Saxon monosyllables: 'What is there?' It
can be answered, moreover, in a word—'Everything.' "

A similar philosophy was expressed in Oscar Mandel's delightful
book, *Chi Po and the Sorcerer: A Chinese Tale for Children and
Philosophers.* [2] In one scene, the boy Chi Po is taking painting
lessons from the sorcerer Bu Fu. At one point, Bu Fu says, "No, no!
You have merely painted what is! Anyone can paint what is; the real
secret is to paint what isn't!" Chi Po, quite puzzled, replies, "But
what is there that isn't?"

Chi Po, though hardly a professional philosopher, was really ex-
pressing the same ontological viewpoint as Professor Quine—
namely, that everything exists, and nothing else exists. Now, some
of the medieval philosophers apparently had quite a different idea;
they believed that existence is a *property* that some things have and
some things don't have, and the nonexistent entities can have lots
of properties despite their nonexistence. So whereas Quine and Chi
Po would agree that there are no centaurs at all—existent or otherwise—these medieval philosophers would say that there *are* centaurs
but no existent ones. In other words, they would say that no centaur
has the property of existence; but that does not imply that there are
no centaurs, for there still can be nonexistent ones.

The philosopher Immanuel Kant vehemently denied that existence is a property, and so Kant, Quine, and Chi Po are in perfect
agreement on this point. Indeed, Kant (though a devout theist)
believed that none of the ontological arguments (which purport to
prove the existence of God by pure reason) were valid because in
all cases they rested on the false assumption that existence is a
property.

Quite frankly, I don't know whether existence is a property or not,
but I am perfectly open to the possibility that it is. I take the

position, however, that even if existence were a property, the onto-logical arguments of Anselm and Descartes are still no good. (I give my reasons for this in item #241 of *What Is the Name of This Book?*,[3] where I show that Descartes' argument proving the existence of God could just as well be used to prove the existence of anything—such as a unicorn.)

A far better version of the ontological argument was given by the unknown Dutch theologian Van Dollard in an unpublished manu-script discovered by Inspector Craig.[4] Van Dollard constructed an axiom system much in the style of the later axiom systems of Spinoza, but his system was far more rigorous! (Sometimes I wonder whether Spinoza ever had access to Van Dollard's writings. Probably not; Spinoza was far too honest not to have mentioned it!) To fully appreciate the subtlety of Van Dollard's thought, I must ask the reader to try to put himself in the frame of mind of the medieval philosophers who believed that existence is a property that some things have and other things do not and that nonexistent things can have various properties just as well as existent things. In Van Dol-lard's system, certain properties are called *perfections,* and a *god* is defined as any being that has all perfections. The system starts with the following two axioms:

Axiom 1. The property of existence is a perfection.

Axiom 2 (the ontological axiom). Given any perfection *P,* if all things having Property *P* also have the property of existence, then there is at least one entity having the Property *P.*

1

From just these two axioms, Van Dollard obtained a rather star-tling result!

Theorem 1 (the ontological theorem). Something exists, that is, there is at least one entity that has the property of existence. (Per-haps Theorem 1 answers Leibniz's question: Why is there some-thing instead of nothing?)

Can the reader see how to prove Theorem 1? (All proofs are given in the appendix to this chapter.)

2

Van Dollard next gave the following two axioms:

Axiom 3. Given any Class C of perfections, the property of having all the perfections in C is again a perfection. (For example, for any two perfections P_1 and P_2, the property of having *both* perfection P_1 *and* perfection P_2 is itself a perfection. The same is true of any three perfections P_1, P_2, P_3, or indeed for *any* class of perfections [whether a finite class or an infinite one]. In modern mathematical terminology, this axiom would be more succinctly stated: The intersection of any class of perfections is a perfection.)[5]

Axiom 4. There is a class of perfections that contains all perfections. (We shall henceforth refer to this class as the *class of all perfections,* and denote it by P.)

From these four axioms, Van Dollard obtained a rather basic theorem in theology:

Theorem 2 (the weak bible theorem). There is at least one god —moreover, an existent one!

To help prove this theorem, Van Dollard first proved as lemmas the following two propositions (which are not without interest in their own right):

Proposition 1 (rediscovered by Descartes). All gods exist, that is, every god has the property of existence.

Proposition 2. The property of being a god is a perfection.

3

This is as far as Van Dollard could get without using the following axiom:

Axiom 5. For any god g, the property of being identical to g is a perfection.

Using this axiom, Van Dollard obtained his major result!

Theorem 3 (the strong bible theorem). There is exactly one God.

Can the reader see how to prove Theorems 2 and 3?

Discussion. Van Dollard's proofs (given in the appendix), unlike the proofs of Anselm and Descartes, are completely rigorous by the most stringent standards of modern logic. Of course, the proofs tell us nothing about whether Axioms 1 through 5 are actually *true,* but as pieces of formal reasoning, they are impeccable! That is to say, whatever meanings one gives to the term *the property of existence* and to the term *perfection, if* the axioms are true under those meanings, *then* Theorems 1 through 3 are also true under those meanings. In other words, Theorems 1 through 3 are really logical consequences of Axioms 1 through 5. Moreover, it is easy to give meanings to those terms under which the axioms *are* true, and so, if nothing more, the axioms are certainly *consistent.*

And What about the Devil?

Good question; what about the devil or devils in general? Are there any? If so, how many are there? Do they have the property of existence? Is it possible that some of them have the property of existence and others not?

Fortunately, all these questions were settled completely in a remarkable manuscript written by a learned church doctor, Alphonso G. (Unfortunately, I am not allowed to divulge his complete name or the name of the manuscript [which, incidentally, was also discovered by Inspector Craig].) The manuscript was branded heretical by the Church, and the author was condemned to be burned at the stake. Fortunately, Alphonso escaped from prison and hid away his precious manuscript—probably the only surviving copy!

It appears from Alphonso's philosophical investigations that there are also certain properties called *antiperfections,* and naturally a *devil* is defined as a being that has all antiperfections. Here are some of Alphonso's postulates concerning antiperfections.

Postulate 1. Nonexistence is an antiperfection. (Nonexistence is of course the property of not having the property of existence.)

Postulate 2. Given any antiperfection A, if there is no existent entity having Property A, then there is no entity at all having Property A. (An existent entity is of course an entity that has the property of existence.)

4

From these two postulates, Alphonso first proved this theorem:

Theorem A. There are no nonexistent entities. In other words: Everything exists! (This means that Quine and Chi Po were right after all!)

Alphonso then proved the following theorem, which may well be the most important theorem ever proved!

Theorem B. There is no devil, existent or otherwise.

Of course it was Theorem B that caused Alphonso's break with the Church.

5

Alphonso had one very talented Polish student, M. Askanas, who (like all of Alphonso's students) believed that there was no devil but would not accept his master's proof. It's not that he believed that there was anything formally wrong with it, but he couldn't bring himself to accept Postulate 2 since it leads to Theorem A, and Askanas was not open to the possibility that there cannot be any nonexistent entities. He therefore proposed an alternative postulate that (with Postulate 1) also yields Theorem B but not Theorem A. Preparatory to stating this postulate, Askanas introduced the following definition: For any Property P, an entity is said to have the Property $P+$ if it has both Property P *and* the property of existence. (For example, if P is the property of being a fruit, then every apple —existent or not—has Property P, but only *existent* apples have the property $P+$.)

Here is Askanas's alternative postulate.

Postulate 2′. For any Antiperfection A, the Property $A+$ is also an antiperfection.

This postulate strikes me as particularly plausible. Indeed, I would say that if A is an antiperfection, then the Property $A+$ is, if anything, even a *worse* antiperfection than $A!$ For example, if A is the property of being a tyrant, isn't the Property $A+$ even worse? That is, isn't an existing tyrant worse than a nonexistent one?

Surely, of the two, the existing tyrant can do the more damage!

Anyhow, as I have said, Theorem B can be derived from Postulate 1 and Postulate 2'. Can the reader see how?

Remarks. Someone once asked me if, instead of proving that there is a God and no devil, couldn't one prove that there is a devil and no God? The answer is: Of course; just change the axioms!

I have heard that in the twelfth century there was a rumor that Alphonso G. had another student who constructed a system that sounds most intriguing! According to the account, this system (like that of Askanas) proved there was no devil and left open the question whether or not there are any nonexistent entities. The system, like that of Van Dollard, proved there was a God—in fact, a unique God—but the most curious thing of all is that the system did *not* prove that there is any *existent* God! In other words, the system proved that there is a unique God, but whether or not God has the property of existence was evidently undecidable in the system. (I'm not sure whether this proposition was *proved* undecidable in the system, or whether it was just that no one was able to decide it.)

This system sounds quite fascinating, and I wish I knew more about it! But, as I have said, it may be only a rumor. Moreover, I'm not sure whether there really was such a rumor, or whether I merely *heard* there was such a rumor.

Medieval Ontology and Solipsism

It has just occurred to me that the medieval ontology that espouses the possibility of nonexistent entities casts a new light on the philosophy of solipsism.

Suppose a solipsist says to me, "I am the only one who exists." How am I to interpret this? From the viewpoint of Quine and Chi Po, the statement can have only one meaning: "There is nobody else but me." But from the viewpoint of medieval ontology, the statement could just as well mean, "I am the only one who has the property of existence."

These two possible meanings strike me as having a drastically different significance. Frankly, I find it almost impossible to believe the solipsist if he intends his statement in the first sense. (I say *almost* for reasons that are dealt with in Chapter 12.) But if the solipsist intends his statement in the second sense, how can I know that he is wrong? Since I don't quite know what this property of existence is, then how can I tell which people have it and which people don't?

Chaudhuri's Ontology

I shouldn't leave the subject of ontology without at least a brief mention of some Eastern thought on the subject.

Many of you have heard the classic Hindu philosophical pronouncement: Nothing exists. Should this be interpreted to mean that no entity has the property of existence or that there are no entities at all?

The only Eastern philosopher I know who has seriously addressed this question is a certain Dr. Chaudhuri (whom I read about in some private notes of Inspector Craig). He vehemently affirmed that the statement was meant only in the *first* sense and that a lot of misunderstanding on the part of Western philosophers was the result of their interpreting it in the second sense. "Of course there are entities," wrote Chaudhuri, "the only question is whether any of them have *reality!*"

I should mention that Chaudhuri translated all of his own works into English and that he used the word *reality* instead of *existence*. He referred to an entity as being either real or unreal, and we shall follow him in this respect. Obviously, he defines a real entity as one that has the property of reality and an unreal entity as one that does not. He stated his main theorem thus:

Theorem C (Chaudhuri's Theorem). Nothing is real.

Chaudhuri derived his theorem from two ontological axioms. He referred to certain properties as Brahmanic properties. (I'm not sure what he meant by a *Brahmanic property*, but I suspect that he meant the same thing as the medieval Western ontologists meant by a *perfection*.) Here are Chaudhuri's ontological axioms.

Axiom C_1. Reality is Brahmanic.[6]

Axiom C_2. Given any Brahmanic property, if there is any real entity having the property, then there is also an unreal one having the property.

From these two axioms, Chaudhuri's theorem easily follows. We leave the proof to the reader.

Appendix

1

Proof of Theorem 1. This is quite simple: Let E be the property of existence. By Axiom 1, E is a perfection. Obviously, anything having Property E has the property of existence (since E *is* the property of existence), and so by Axiom 2, there is something having Property E, that is, there is something having the property of existence.

2

We first prove Propositions 1 and 2.

Proof of Proposition 1. This proposition is a trivial one and follows from Axiom 1 alone: Let g be any god; g has all perfections. By Axiom 1, the property of existence is a perfection. Therefore, g has the property of existence.

Proof of Proposition 2. This proposition follows from Axioms 3 and 4: Let P be the class of all perfections. (There is such a class by Axiom 3.) Let G be the property of being a god. By the definition of a god, Property G is nothing more nor less than the property of having all the perfections in P. Then by Axiom 4, this Property G is a perfection.

Proof of Theorem 2. Again, let G be the property of being a god. By Proposition 1, every entity having Property G has the property of existence (this is the same thing as saying that all gods have the property of existence). Also, by Proposition 2, the Property G is a perfection. Then by Axiom 2, there must be at least one entity having Property G, which means that there is at least one god.

3

Proof of Theorem 3. We have already proved that there is at least one god, so all that remains to prove is that there is at most one god.[7]

Let g_1 be any god. We will prove that given any god g_2, it must be that g_2 is identical with g_1. Suppose that g_2 is a god. Since g_1 is a god, then by Axiom 5 the property of being identical to g_1 is a perfection. But g_2, being a god, has *all* perfections, so in particular, g_2 has the perfection of being identical to g_1. This proves that any gods g_1, g_2 must be identical, and hence there cannot be more than one god.

4

Proof of Theorem A. Let N be the property of nonexistence. It is obvious that nothing having Property N can also have the property of existence. Then by Postulate 2 there is no entity at all having Property N. In other words, there is no entity at all having the property of nonexistence. (This proof uses Postulate 2, but it does not require Postulate 1!)

Proof of Theorem B. From Postulate 1 alone it follows that there cannot be any *existing* devil (which is already a relief!) because by definition every devil has all antiperfections, and nonexistence is an antiperfection (by Postulate 1), and so every devil has the property of nonexistence. So if there were a devil, it would have the property of nonexistence. But by Theorem A, there is no entity at all that can have the property of nonexistence. Hence, there is no devil.

5

Askanas's Proof of Theorem B. Askanas's proof is a bit more subtle! We recall that we now have Postulate 1 and Postulate 2' available but not Postulate 2.

Again let N be the property of nonexistence. Since we don't have Postulate 2 available, we cannot conclude that no entity has Property N. However, by Postulate 1, the Property N *is* an antiperfection. Then by Postulate 2', the Property $N+$ is also an antiperfection. Now, nothing can possibly have Property $N+$ (because such an entity would have both the Property N of nonexistence and the property of existence, and this is a contradiction). But since $N+$ is an antiperfection, then if there *were* a devil, it would have to have Property $N+$. Therefore, there is no devil.

Notes

1. Richard Wincor, *Sherlock Holmes in Tibet* (New York: Weybright and Talley, 1968).

2. Oscar Mandel, *Chi Po and the Sorcerer: A Chinese Tale for Children and Philosophers* (Tokyo: Charles E. Tuttle Co., 1964).

3. Raymond Smullyan, *What Is the Name of This Book?* (Englewood Cliffs, N.J.: Prentice-Hall, 1977).

4. This is the same Inspector Craig of whom I wrote so much in *The Lady Or The Tiger?* (New York: Alfred A. Knopf, 1982).

5. Parenthetical remarks accompanying the axioms are mine.

6. If my aforementioned suspicion is correct, then except for terminology this axiom is the same as Van Dollard's first axiom.

7. This, according to a famous quip of Alfred North Whitehead, is the creed of the Unitarians.

5

Concluding Pieces

11

Dream or Reality?

To distinguish the real from the unreal, one must experience them both.

S. Gorn's *Compendium of Rarely Used Clichés* [1]

SKEPTIC: You claim that you see a chair. How do you know that you see a chair?

SUBJECT: I never said that I know that I see a chair; I merely said that I *see* a chair. I am not as sure that I know that I see a chair as I am that I see a chair. To me, seeing is more immediate than knowing.

SKEPTIC: Suppose I prove to you that you don't see a chair?

SUBJECT: No proof can convince me since I already know that I do see a chair.

SKEPTIC: Ah, I've caught you! You do claim you *know* you see a chair.

SUBJECT: I never denied knowing it; I merely said that I am less sure that I know it than that I am seeing the chair.

SKEPTIC: And you would still claim to see the chair even if I proved to you that you don't?

SUBJECT: Of course I would!

SKEPTIC: Then you are being irrational.

SUBJECT: Not really.

SKEPTIC: Can you prove that you are seeing a chair?

SUBJECT: Of course not! Or rather, I should ask, "Prove it from what premises?"

SKEPTIC: Can you at least prove that it is probable?

SUBJECT: Probable? I don't even know what it means to say that it is *probable* that I am seeing a chair. What I say is that I *am* seeing a chair.

SKEPTIC: But how do you know that you are seeing a chair?

SUBJECT: You asked me that before. Let me say this: First of all, I am not completely clear that I understand the meaning of *how I know* anymore than *how I see.* But to the extent that I do understand it, I can honestly say that I do not know *how* I know that I see a chair.

SKEPTIC: So you don't know *how* you know you see a chair, and you admit you can't prove you see a chair, yet you stubbornly maintain that you see a chair.

SUBJECT: Of course!

SKEPTIC: Then you are being dogmatic!

SUBJECT: Perhaps.

SKEPTIC: But do you really want to be dogmatic? Just think of what dogma leads to! Think of fascism, communism, and the Spanish Inquisition.

SUBJECT: Oh, come on now; these are examples of intolerance, not just dogmatism!

SKEPTIC: But what is the difference between dogmatism and intolerance?

SUBJECT: The present case is as good an illustration as any. One might label my dogged belief that I see a chair *dogmatic* (though I am not sure this would be correct), but surely no one in his right mind would label this belief of mine *an act of intolerance!*

SKEPTIC: The reason that I cannot accept your statement that you see a chair is that I doubt the existence of chairs. I think, however, that one can translate your statement into another form whose truth I would accept. I think that what you are *really* trying to say is that you are having a certain visual sensation—the so-called sensation of seeing a chair.

SUBJECT: If it makes you happy to translate it into those terms, by all means do so! *I* would not think of saying it this way. It *may* be also true—in fact, it probably is true—that I am having this so-called sensation. But again, as I see it, the notion of sensation is a far more sophisticated concept than just seeing and leads to a considerable number of philosophical problems and ambiguities. To a phenomenalist or idealist, a sensation is an immediate element of experience. To a materialistic realist, a sensation is a certain brain state or cerebral phenomenon, which seems to me to be something completely different. At any rate, the sort of statements that I most immediately understand are things like, "I see a chair," "I see a table," and so forth. I understand statements involving terms like *sensation* mainly to the extent to which I can translate them into such primitive statements.

SKEPTIC: But would it not be a more secure basis for philosophy to start out assuming only the things one really knows, like one's own sensations? No one but you can know whether you have a sensation or not. So if you say you have a given sensation, it cannot be reasonably denied. But you have absolutely no basis for claiming to know that the sensation is *of* something.

SUBJECT: This whole way of starting out philosophy is, to my mind, the worst one possible. To start out with one's *sensations* (or sense data) as the primary known realities! Children, who to my mind are the best philosophers, don't do anything like that. They talk about *objects*, not *sensations* of objects. Once you start out with sensations as the given, then you get involved in the whole nightmare of worrying about the very problem you raised: Are there objects corresponding to these sensations, or are there just free-floating sensations, so to speak? Then the problem arises as to what these objects are really like: How do they resemble our sensations of them, how do they cause the sensations of them, and for that matter what real evidence do we have for their very existence? Is our evidence probabilistic, or must we accept objects as an act of "animal faith"? Kant thought it a scandal of philosophy that the existence of external objects had never been satisfactorily proved. But to me, the search for a proof is utterly ridiculous. I directly perceive the objects; what more could I want? I don't *perceive* sensations at all. At least, the things I perceive I don't call *sensations* but *objects*, like this chair. I can assure you that if I did not perceive this chair directly, then absolutely *no* proof for its existence would carry the slightest conviction with me. I honestly regard it as pathological to require proofs of things one already knows.

An important consideration has just occurred to me. There is another way—a totally different way—of understanding the statement, "I see a chair," than the one I had in mind, that is, the way it would be understood by a physicist qua physicist, which is a statement about the physical world, made within the framework of physics. This *secondary* interpretation, which to my utter amazement is regarded as primary by some philosophers, states that my body is now facing the chair, I am awake with open eyes, light rays are reflected from the chair that form an image on my retina, causing physiological changes in my optic nerve, brain, and so forth. If this "physicalistic" interpretation of my statement is what you understood, then I can well understand your labeling my sureness of it an unfounded dogma—indeed, I would agree! I *believe* that this secondary interpretation also holds, but I cannot possibly *know* it in the absolute sense that I know the other. Indeed, I know this only secondhand, that is, on the testimony of scientists. I have never seen my brain or optic nerve and only know of them from authorities I trust. Incidentally, my objections to analyzing the statement, "I see a chair," into objects and relationships does not apply to the "physicalistic" interpretation; indeed, this interpretation does put together things like human bodies, chairs, light rays, optic nerves, brains, and so forth. Although I also clearly understand this secondary interpretation, it is a far more involved business than the primary interpretation, and I am able to understand this secondary interpretation only by analyzing it ultimately in terms of experience statements in their primary sense.

SKEPTIC: Since you make this sharp dichotomy between what you call the primary and secondary interpretations of experience statements and claim such an important difference between them, how in discourse do you make clear which meaning you have in mind?

SUBJECT: With philosophers—particularly so-called materialists—this is usually the most difficult thing in the world! With most people —especially with children—there is no difficulty whatsoever since they usually understand experience sentences only in the primary sense. Of course, primitive people—as well as all people who lived before the rise of science and so knew nothing about optic nerves and brains—can understand such statements *only* in the primary sense.

The situation seems to me well-nigh tragic. People in their childhood understand only the primary interpretation of experience statements. But at some stage of their development, particularly those who study science, they become aware of the secondary interpretation. They learn that one sees a chair when and only when one's physical brain is in a certain state. This is an exciting realization. But unfortunately certain people—those who become materialists—tend to identify the two meanings and cannot subsequently separate them. It may be possible that they even forget after awhile the primary meaning altogether, but I think this in fact unlikely. If they did, it almost would be too frightening to imagine. It would be as if someone like Alberecht traded love for gold, and after living in the world of gold for awhile totally forgot what love was even like except in the purely operational sense of understanding how people behave when they are in love. But as I said, I doubt that my fears have any real basis. To use an analogy, a blind physicist knows what the word *red* means only in the *secondary* sense; a sighted child, knowing no physics, knows the word in the *primary* sense. I doubt very much if a sighted adult who became blind could ever in his lifetime actually forget what *red* meant in the primary sense.

SKEPTIC: Isn't it unfortunate that the same words and phrases have these two very different senses and that our language doesn't have separate phrases for the two meanings?

SUBJECT: Extremely unfortunate! This is precisely one of the things that leads to so much confusion in philosophy!

SKEPTIC: Is there no way that you can explain your distinction of primary and secondary meanings of experience statements to, say, a hard-boiled materialist?

SUBJECT: They are obviously aware that I think that there are two meanings. The secondary meaning they already understand (at least I think they do). As for the primary meaning, those who are polite say, "I have no idea what you could possibly mean"; those who are more crass say, "You don't mean *anything at all;* you are just using meaningless words, you are simply talking nonsense!"

SKEPTIC: Could you give me an example?

SUBJECT: Yes. One way I can explain that my primary meaning of, "I see a chair," is totally different from the secondary meaning is this: Under the secondary meaning, it would be a total contradiction in terms to say that I might see a chair after my bodily death. But under the primary meaning, there is no contradiction at all. Whether I will see chairs after my death is (to my mind) simply an unknown fact, but it is inconceivable to me that the notion is *contradictory.* I am thinking of Schlick, who maintained that in principle there is no reason why he should not witness his own funeral. Ayer, on the other hand, held this notion to be self-contradictory. Clearly, Schlick was thinking of witnessing in what I term the primary sense, Ayer in the secondary sense. Obviously, Ayer would not accept my argument at all; he would not agree that his difference with Schlick showed that there are *two* senses of the phrase *I see* or *I witness.* He would deny that what I call the primary sense has any meaning at all.

SKEPTIC: Tell me, would you commit yourself to saying that you *know* that you see a chair?

SUBJECT: Yes, I would.

SKEPTIC: You realize, of course, that this commits you to saying that you know that you are now not dreaming.

SUBJECT: Not at all!

SKEPTIC: What!

SUBJECT: I said, "Not at all." I regard it as perfectly possible that right now I *am* dreaming.

SKEPTIC: Good God! Surely if you are dreaming right now, then you don't still maintain that you *now* see a chair!

SUBJECT: I most certainly do! In a million years, I would not *dream* of making my assertion that I see a chair dependent on the fact that I'm not dreaming.

SKEPTIC: But if you are now dreaming, then the chair you claim to see *doesn't even exist!*

SUBJECT: It most certainly *does* exist; I *see* it! It is one of the objects I am now dreaming about (assuming that I am actually dreaming).

SKEPTIC: But surely you don't maintain that the objects you dreamed about, say, last night, really exist!

SUBJECT: They may not exist now, but they sure as hell existed last night; I *saw* them!

SKEPTIC: No, no; you are putting it the wrong way! It's not that last night you *really* saw *dream* objects; it's that last night you *dreamed* that you saw *real* objects, but in fact you were wrong!

SUBJECT: Not at all; last night I really saw objects.

SKEPTIC: Would you call these objects real or not?

SUBJECT: This brings us to the heart of the matter. Look, I don't use such words as *real, unreal, dream, nondream, real world, unreal world* in an absolute sense but only in a relative sense. Let me explain.

What do I mean when I say that right now I may be dreaming? This should be explained first. Well, last night I went to sleep and then saw all sorts of objects. This morning I woke up, and where are all these objects? They are nowhere to be found in the world I now experience. So I tend to declare them unreal and the state I was in last night a "dream state," or the world I experienced last night a dream world. When I say that I may be dreaming now, all I mean is that I am open to the possibility that at some future time I may be in a state in which I regard my present state as I did my state last night. In other words, the experience of having gone from one state into another, in which the former state seemed to be unreal, has happened to me many times, and I cannot see why it cannot happen to me again with regard to the very state I am in now. It could be that in the next day or hour I could again have the experience I call *waking up* and regard my present state as unreal. In fact, I don't expect this to happen the next hour, day, week, month, or several years. But when my body dies, I am less sure that I will not enter a state relative to which my present state is a dream. And this state in turn may prove to be unreal relative to some future state, and so forth ad infinitum.

At any rate, I no longer believe in any absolute notion of what is real. I only think of the reality of a state or of an object as relative to some other state. Thus, the very question of whether I am now dreaming in some absolute sense is (to me) meaningless. I can only consider such a purely empirical question as whether or not my present state will one day seem unreal. Every state is real relative to itself. To me, it is an open question whether or not every state may be unreal relative to some other state.[2]

SKEPTIC: I must say, your idea terrifies me! Look, before we started talking about dreams, I thought that the whole time you were defending the philosophy of common sense in an uninhibitedly dogmatic manner. You *see* chairs; therefore, there *are* chairs, and so forth. Then you pull this complete reversal and come up with this ultrafantastic *idealism!* I must say, I am completely bewildered, and it will take me awhile to get over the shock.

SUBJECT: I don't regard this idea as either fantastic or idealistic.

SKEPTIC: Of course it is idealistic to say that *nothing* has absolute reality, that reality is only *relative* to something else!

SUBJECT: This is not idealism.

SKEPTIC: Look, I'm not going to quibble with you over terminology. Maybe it shouldn't be called *idealism* but simply *crazy and fantastic.* All right, I admit that on purely logical grounds, your position is no more disprovable than, say, something like solipsism. At least, at the moment I am not clever enough to find an actual inconsistency in your doctrine. So on rational grounds, I cannot refute you. But on psychological grounds I find the doctrine extremely dangerous. Frankly, the idea that one day I might wake up or be in another state relative to which all the objects and people around me that I have come to know and love should turn out to be *unreal* fills me with utter horror and totally shatters my feelings of security.

SUBJECT: I am glad that you brought up psychological factors because I think that they are most relevant. My psychological reaction is the very opposite of yours; to me, the belief in some absolute reality would make *me* highly insecure!

SKEPTIC: Why on earth should it do that?

SUBJECT: Because once I believed in this thing called *reality*, then I would start worrying about whether the things that appeared real to me really were real!

SKEPTIC: Why can't you just *know* that they are real as I do?

SUBJECT: Hey, I thought *you* were the skeptic! It seems in some ways that I am more skeptical than you.

SKEPTIC: You sure are! Indeed, your whole method of philosophizing is the strangest mixture of dogmatism and skepticism I have ever seen! About certain things you are totally dogmatic and about all other things—all things that are not *your* dogmas—you are skeptical.

SUBJECT: But of course! How could I be anything other than dogmatic about things that I know and skeptical about things that I don't?

SKEPTIC: But tell me honestly, why are you skeptical that the things before you are real in any absolute sense?

SUBJECT: When you use the word *why*, I am not sure whether you are asking for a psychological explanation as to how I got this way, or whether you are asking for my epistemological reasons. Let me first consider the former, which brings us back to the very important point you raised about feeling secure. Don't you see that once I admitted an absolute reality, I would have all the nightmarish problems about whether I am *really* awake or not. But without this category, all these awful problems don't even arise!

SKEPTIC: But ignoring a problem does not solve it! I can't reject the notion of reality just to avoid facing problems. Besides, the very thought that there is no such thing as reality itself makes me insecure.

SUBJECT: Originally, you told me that my philosophy, though possibly consistent, was dangerous because it leads to psychological insecurity. In other words, your immediate reason for rejecting it was that it makes *you* feel insecure. But now when I tell you that it makes *me* feel secure, you say these are not legitimate grounds for accepting it. Are you being quite fair?

SKEPTIC: No, you are right.

SUBJECT: I would like to say more about feeling secure. It is difficult for me to believe that what really makes you (or me, for that matter) feel insecure is that the objects we both see lack this property of absolute reality. Isn't the real fear that at some future time we may come to believe or to *feel* the unreality of the objects we both now perceive?

SKEPTIC: That is certainly part of it, but not all.

SUBJECT: Well, let me put it this way. Suppose God himself (or any being you would take to be both omniscient and truthful) would now come down to earth and say to you, "There is indeed such a thing as absolute reality. But, for certain reasons, I am not going to tell you whether any of the things or people you now perceive are real. This much I promise you, however: Never will you have the experience of one day being in a state relative to which your present state will appear like a dream. In other words, if you are dreaming now, then—unlike the dreams you have had before—you will never know it, not even in the afterlife, if there is one." My question now is whether this answer would satisfy you.

SKEPTIC: I'm afraid not. This would mean that I never would know which things were real and which were not.

SUBJECT: Well, suppose God then said, "All right, I'll tell you after all. Everything you now see *is* real." Would that satisfy you?

SKEPTIC: It would still not satisfy me, because I might be afraid that I was only dreaming that God spoke to me.

SUBJECT: Hey, it seems that *you* are the one who is *really* insecure! Insecure, that is, in *your* philosophy, not mine!

SKEPTIC: I'm afraid you are right. Well, I guess what I need is to have *faith* that I am now not dreaming.

SUBJECT: Ah! That is precisely the difference between your approach and mine. I don't want my feeling of security to have to depend on any act of faith. I have always thought of faith as somehow "whistling in the dark."

SKEPTIC: But how without some act of faith can you know you are not now dreaming?

SUBJECT: I told you before that I use the word *dream* only in a relative sense. But a point that I think may be important has just occurred to me. When I suggest the possibility that reality is only relative, that every world (or state) may be unreal relative to some other world, does this idea make you feel that the present world (the one we are now in and see) is less real than you would normally feel, or that other worlds are more real? In other words, do you feel that

I am trying to make the present world more fantasylike, dreamlike, or chimerical or that I am trying to make fantasy worlds appear more real?

SKEPTIC: Why, the former, of course. If I believed that every world was unreal relative to some other world, then I would feel that *all* worlds, including this one, were unreal.

SUBJECT: Oh, if that is your reaction, then I certainly don't blame you for totally rejecting the idea. I was thinking of it the opposite way! I was not trying to "derealify" this world but rather to "realify" so-called nonreal worlds. Why can't you see it in this light?

SKEPTIC: I don't know; the idea is quite new to me. I would have to think about it.

SUBJECT: You see, there is one important difference in our attitudes. Suppose for the moment that there really is an afterlife and that in the first state we enter the present world is unreal relative to that state. Your reaction will be very different from mine. You will say, "How surprising; I thought my previous state was real, but I was wrong; I was *deceived.*" I will say, "Just as I thought, the last state was real and interesting while it lasted, but was *impermanent.* Too bad, I guess nothing lasts forever."

I really think that the notion of permanence is the key to the whole business. Let me ask you another question. Suppose you were on another planet—call it Planet *A*—on which all the inhabitants, including yourself, slept half the time (instead of roughly a third of the time, as we do here). Now suppose at the end of each day on Planet *A* you undressed, went to bed, fell asleep, and found yourself in a totally different body—call it Body *B*—on a totally different planet called Planet *B*. You would spend a day on Planet *B*, at the end of which your *B*-body would undress, get into bed, go to sleep, and then you would return to State *A*. Let us assume that your existence in State *B* were just as consistent and coherent as in State *A*. When in State *A* you put some object on the desk and went to sleep, the next morning it was still there, and the same held for State *B*. Assume also that this state of affairs has been going on all your life; indeed, you were unable to recall whether your life started in

State *A* or State *B*. I repeat, each state had the same coherent internal structure. Let us say that science and psychology were about equally advanced in both worlds. The scientists of World *A* would assure you that your thought processes were nothing more nor less than certain physiological events in your brain—call it Brain *A*. They would tell you that when you went to sleep and "dreamed" you were on Planet *B*, this "dream" was nothing more than certain physical events taking place in Brain *A*. But the scientists of Planet *B* would tell you exactly the same thing in reverse; all your thoughts were nothing but events in Brain *B*. Moreover, they would tell you that Brain *A* doesn't really exist at all; those on Planet *A* would tell you that Brain *B* doesn't really exist except as a figment of the imagination of Brain *A*. I can even imagine the psychiatrists of both planets each diagnosing you as schizophrenic for believing in the reality of the other state; perhaps each would offer you some medication that would permanently cure you of your "illusion" concerning the other state.

Now, you must admit that under these circumstances your whole notion of reality would probably be very different. What would you believe? That either State *A* or State *B* was real and the other illusory, but you couldn't decide which? Or maybe that both states were real—that there could be, so to speak, two disjoint realities? Or perhaps you would suspect that both states were unreal and that your *real* state—State *C*—was something very different yet? Or maybe that *no* states are real? Don't you think that you would reject the very notion of reality as meaningless and would simply settle for the realization that each of the two states was internally real but that neither one was real relative to the other and that the only common bond would be that you experience them both?

SKEPTIC: Of course, *had* I lived such a life, my views on reality would probably have been very different. But the fact is that I have *not* lived such a weird life. So why should I let my views be influenced by the hypothetical situation you have just been spinning out, which itself is just a sheer fantasy? I'd like to know what you are really driving at. Tell me honestly, why are you so intent on trying to relativize the notion of reality? You said before something about having some epistemological reasons for rejecting any absolute notion of reality. What now are these reasons?

SUBJECT: My reason for rejecting it is very simply that I have absolutely no reasons for accepting it. Indeed, I don't even know what the notion really means! I have no idea how I can use the notion. Suppose I enter a new place and see a wooden chair. At least it *looks* wooden to me, but then it occurs to me that it may not be really wooden; perhaps it is cleverly painted papier mâché. In this sense, the word *really* means something quite definite to me; I know how to go about testing it. So I go over to the chair, inspect it more closely, feel it, and so forth, and conclude, "Yes, it really is made of wood." But now, what in the world would it mean for me to ask, "But is this chair real, or is it only illusory?" What test can I possibly perform to find out if the chair has this mysterious property of being real?

SKEPTIC: Why is it that you, who are usually so hostile to positivism, take such a positivist attitude toward this question?

SUBJECT: Because in this regard, I feel that the positivists have something of value to contribute. Incidentally, concerning my "hostile" attitude toward positivism, I think that I should state clearly that I divide positivists into two types, which I call *dogmatic positivists* and *skeptical positivists*. The dogmatic positivist will say about any word, phrase, or sentence whose meaning he cannot understand that it is meaningless or nonsensical. The skeptical positivist will instead be skeptical that it has any meaning or will wonder what the meaning could be. I am perfectly sympathetic to the skeptical positivist; it is only the dogmatic positivist of whom I am totally intolerant. After all, since I am dogmatic myself, it is only natural that I cannot tolerate any dogmas that conflict with mine.

But coming back to the notion of absolute reality, I, like the skeptical positivist, do not really understand what the notion is and indeed have some doubts that the notion has any real meaning. But I am not prepared to say that it is meaningless. The notion of absolute reality somehow reminds me of the notion of absolute position in space or absolute motion in space. When people first hear from the physical relativist that there is no such thing as bodies moving through something called *space,* but that bodies move only relative to each other, the reaction is often something of a shock; the new idea somehow seems counterintuitive. The dogmatic type of relativist will say, "There is no such thing as absolute motion; this is just an antiquated notion." The more modest and reasonable type of relativist, when asked, "How do you know that there is no such thing as absolute motion through space?" will reply, "I cannot say for sure that there is no such thing but merely that I do not know what it is and can see no possible way to use it in science. The subject matter of physical science is simply the description of how objects move relative to each other. And nowhere can I see how the hypothesis of absolute motion can be used in this study."

I have similar feelings about a chair's being real. Saying that it is relatively real is quite different. Again, this notion is related to the notion of permanence. I will put it this way: I certainly do have a notion of something appearing real or seeming real to me. For example, the chair I see before me certainly seems real to me. The chair I saw yesterday while I was awake seemed real to me then and still seems real to me in retrospect. But the objects I saw last night in my sleep seemed real to me then (at least as far as I now remember) but do not seem real to me now. So it is perfectly meaningful to ask whether I may *in the future* be in a state in which the chair I presently perceive will then seem unreal to me.

SKEPTIC: But this again is something you cannot now test.

SUBJECT: Of course I can't possibly test the chair to find out whether *in the future* it will seem real to me any more than I can now test it to determine whether in the future some rock will be hurled through the window and demolish it.[3] But both notions seem to me perfectly meaningful.

SKEPTIC: Perhaps your idea of relative reality is not so bad after all. It also may not be a bad idea to define something to be absolutely real to a given observer if it is in your sense permanently real, that is, if at no future time will it seem unreal.

Still, I am vaguely disquieted. I must say that I have a lingering intuition that there is something more to reality than a mere reduction to a permanent set of appearances. Do you honestly maintain that you have *no* such intuition?

SUBJECT: To be absolutely honest, I do have such a lingering intuition. But for that matter, I must also confess that I still have left *some* remnants of my childhood intuition concerning absolute motion.

SKEPTIC: So how do you reconcile these intuitions with your relativist position?

SUBJECT: I, as it were, hold such intuitions in abeyance. Incidentally, my intuition concerning absolute motion is much weaker than my intuition concerning absolute reality. Indeed, by now it has practically disappeared. But with the notion of absolute reality I am less sure that there is nothing to it. What should one do with such intuitions, intuitions that conflict with reason or with stronger intuitions? I do not believe in being overly brutal and harsh—even with oneself—and tearing out those intuitions that one regretfully realizes are not in complete harmony with one's general world view. I have far too much respect for *any* intuition to wish to "murder" it. So I let such intuitions, so to speak, lie asleep. I say to myself, "It is difficult to know what absolute reality can be, other than what I have suggested. But then again it appears possibly to have some other meaning. But I don't know how to work with such a meaning. So I will suspend final judgment until I have more knowledge."

SKEPTIC: I think your attitude is very reasonable. Still, I would love to know just a little more about your intuition of absolute reality. Strange, isn't it, that *I* have been defending this notion, and you have been attacking it. Yet you have so convinced me that this notion is unsatisfactory that I have to appeal to *you* for help in finding out what *I* mean by *absolutely real!* What is it you are looking for, and how will you recognize it if you ever find out? Or do you feel that in principle you never can?

SUBJECT: No, I would not say that in principle I never can find it, though I have as yet no idea of how I can or even just what it is that I seek. I am not one to go along with the idea that it is hopeless to find something unless one knows precisely what it is that one is looking for. So it is with the notion of absolute reality. I told you all my skeptical reasons for doubting that there is really anything to this notion, and so I am unable to use it in my actual life. Yet, as I have confessed, I still sometimes have the haunting feeling that I am overlooking something crucial, that I may be missing something of extreme importance. How can I find it? God only knows! There is nothing more at present that I can possibly do. But who knows? Maybe one day the idea, if there really is any idea, might dawn on me. Perhaps through further advance of science, through a more refined logical analysis of the question, or through something like a sudden mystical insight, it might happily happen that I will say, "Ah, of course! How simple! So that's what reality *really* is!"

Notes

1. S. Gorn, *Compendium of Rarely Used Clichés* (unpublished and used with permission of the author).
2. To the mathematical reader, the situation as described has a resemblance to conclusions some mathematical logicians have drawn from the Skolem-Löwenheim theorem. This theorem is to the effect that no axiom system (of first order logic) can compel the domain of interpretation to be nondenumerable. This led Skolem and others to believe that the very notion of nondenumerability has no absolute meaning.
3. This reminds me of the beautiful Haiku poem:

> There is nothing in the voice of the cicada
> To indicate how long it will live.

12

Enlightened Solipsism

ANDRICUS: I can well imagine why some Eastern mystics and philosophers find so strange our Western idea that one *should* love and treat one's neighbor as oneself. I am thinking of the type who believes that one's neighbor *is* oneself! Naturally, someone who believes this needs nothing like ethics or morality to treat others well but would do so for the very same reasons that one treats oneself well. Under this belief, the very notion of sacrifice would be meaningless. This is an interesting example of how a purely metaphysical hypothesis can have fundamental ethical ramifications without appealing at all to anything like principles of morality.

MORALIST: It would be a fine kettle of fish if people had to have *such* an idea to behave ethically!

FIRST PHILOSOPHER: This idea only substantiates what I have always said, namely, that if you start out with nonsense, you usually end up with nonsense! The hypothesis that my neighbor *is* myself is so patently absurd that it seems an utter waste of time to even consider its further ramifications.

ANDRICUS: But I ask, is it all that absurd? Does it have no meaning whatsoever? Even if strictly speaking it is false (or even meaningless), may it not at least suggest something of value that perhaps a more conventionally meaningful sentence would not suggest?[1]

SECOND PHILOSOPHER: If you claim that there is any meaning in the sentence, "My neighbor is myself," then it is incumbent on you to demonstrate this fact!

FIRST PHILOSOPHER: Three cheers!

ANDRICUS: Softly, my friends! I make no claim whatsoever. I feel, however, that there is something extremely important in this sentence. All I wish to do is to discuss with you certain ideas that have occurred to me in the process of trying to understand it. Before this, however, I wish to mention a closely related point. Many people feel that this is an unjust world since some lives are fraught with so much suffering and others with so much joy.

FIRST PHILOSOPHER: Obviously! Everybody in his right mind knows that.

ANDRICUS: Well now, consider a hundred booths in a building, each one containing an occupant watching a private movie. Suppose some of the movies are very good and others very bad. At first sight, this situation seems very unjust; why should some be more privileged than others to see good movies? But suppose upon learning more about the setup we found out that the overall plan was that the occupants were to rotate, and hence everyone would see all one hundred movies, but each in a different order. Then we would revise our opinion about the situation's being unjust.

FIRST PHILOSOPHER: This is obviously an analogy; what are you driving at?

ANDRICUS: It seems to me that it is logically possible that the physical universe simply repeats its history over and over again and that we sentient beings (minds, souls, egos, spirits, psyches, call us what you will) simply interchange roles, that is, each of us inhabits the body of some living organism during one universal cycle; in the next cycle, we switch organisms. Thus, we all "see the same show" but in different orders. If this were true, then clearly the world would *not* be unjust.

FIRST PHILOSOPHER: *If* this were true; that's a pretty big if.

ANDRICUS: I am not claiming the hypothesis to be true; I am only claiming it to be *possible*. If I am not wrong in this claim, then an important conclusion can be drawn: Some pessimists claim that the existing world is *necessarily* unjust; there is no possible way of justifying it. Now, if my hypothesis is true, then the world is not unjust. Hence, if my hypothesis is possible (which no one has yet disproved), then it is possible that the world is not unjust, and hence the pessimists' claim that the world is necessarily unjust is false.

SECOND PHILOSOPHER: The world obviously *is* unjust, and it is clearly up to *us* to make the world *more* just! Your theory constitutes the perfect apology for the quietist who wishes to sit back and let things remain as bad as they are. Just think! If your theory were true, then the world would already be perfectly just and would remain perfectly just in the future regardless of what we did. In other words, there is nothing we could do to make the world any more just, so we might as well sit back and continue in our rotten ways!

ANDRICUS: Ah, but that is precisely my second point! Just think, if my hypothesis were true—or more important, if it were generally believed—how much better would we treat each other! My neighbor's fortunes and misfortunes are nothing more than my own past or future fortunes and misfortunes.

MORALIST: At this point, I vigorously protest! Apart from the utter metaphysical absurdity of the hypothesis, I vehemently deny that its *belief* would lead to more moral behavior! I wish to categorically state once and for all that if I refrained from hurting my neighbor simply because I believed that I would one day be hurting myself, then my act would have no moral worth whatsoever.

ANDRICUS: Well now, that depends upon one's basic orientation toward morality. Tell me, are you a Christian?

MORALIST: Yes.

ANDRICUS: Well, does not Christianity motivate people toward good deeds by talk of rewards and punishments in a future life? Would you regard it of no moral worth for a man to try to live a good life to obtain salvation or escape damnation?

MORALIST: Of course God metes out punishments and rewards in the afterlife. But the truly moral man does not pursue the good for the *purpose* of obtaining rewards or avoiding punishments; he pursues the good only for the sake of the good.

ANDRICUS: You grant that Bishop Berkeley was a good Christian apologist?

MORALIST: Of course!

ANDRICUS: Well, perhaps you are aware that in his essay, "Future Rewards and Punishments," he actually stated that a man who did not believe in future rewards and punishments would act a *foolish* part in being honest. He continued,

> For what reason is there why such a one should postpone his own private interest or pleasure in doing his duty? . . . But he that, having no such view, should yet conscientiously deny himself a present good in any incident where he may save appearances is altogether as *stupid* as he that would trust him at such a juncture.[2]

MORALIST: I am aware that Berkeley unfortunately wrote these words. Look, I certainly regard Berkeley as a model Christian in almost all respects. But this particular sentiment I regard as most un-Christian! Christianity in the true sense of the word teaches that though moral acts do carry future rewards, one should perform them not for the sake of the rewards but simply because they are right. This was clearly recognized by Immanuel Kant. Indeed, Kant had the insight to realize that even when one performed a helpful act for a neighbor merely out of sympathy or compassion, the act had no moral worth since it was then performed only out of *identification* with one's neighbor's feelings, and hence, in the last analysis, only done out of consideration for one's own feelings. In other words, such an act is only a disguised form of selfishness.

ANDRICUS: Oh come now, if you carry that type of analysis far enough, then any action can be regarded as another form of selfishness. It could be equally argued that your very attachment to what you call *morality* is only a form of selfishness; in other words, you perform moral actions only because of the satisfaction you get from doing what you know to be right.

MORALIST: I protest! This is an old and vicious hedonist trick. The hedonists try to rationalize their selfishness at any costs; obviously, they cannot successfully do so. Hence, to assuage their guilt feelings for their selfishness (which shines through their philosophy however they may try to hide it), they point an accusing finger at the decent moralist and claim that he is just as selfish as they!

ANDRICUS: I think that you misunderstood the point I was trying to make. I was not claiming that your pursuit of the good is not moral but only that if your argument were correct, then it could also be turned against you. In other words, I was merely attempting a sort of reductio ad absurdum argument against your position. I know that some hedonists also do this, and though I am definitely not a hedonist, I think that they are right in this respect. In other words, if you are going to bring moral charges against hedonists—even those who act altruistically not out of moral principle but simply out of human kindness—if you charge them with selfishness for doing this, I do not see how the same charge cannot be leveled against you for the pursuit of morality itself.

MORALIST: But there is all the world of difference between the two.

ANDRICUS: Is there really? I guess your point is that virtue is its own reward and that one should pursue virtue only for the very reward implicit in virtue itself.

MORALIST: No, that is still not right. One should not pursue virtue for *any* reward whatsoever—not even the reward implicit in virtue itself. Of course, I believe that virtue is its own reward but that does not mean that one should pursue it for the sake of that reward. One should pursue virtue only for its own sake.

ANDRICUS: I think you are demanding something that in principle is impossible. You are essentially demanding that a person do something without having *any* motivation whatsoever. It is as if you were saying, "I want you to do this; but I don't want you to *want* to do it!" You are really giving contradictory commands—you are placing your listener in a double bind. The effect on a sensitive person can be psychologically shattering in the extreme. I think it is this aspect of so-called morality that more than any other has given rise to such strong antimoral feelings in the world.

FIRST PHILOSOPHER: How did we ever get sidetracked on the subject of morality? On moral grounds I am afraid I agree with Andricus rather than the moralist. I am basically a utilitarian and a pragmatist. I fully agree that if either the mystical hypothesis, "Your neighbor is yourself," or Andricus's hypothesis, "Your neighbor is your past or future self," were generally believed, then certainly people would treat each other far better than they do now, and this would indeed make for a better world. Whether moral worth should then be imputed to their motives, I leave for the moral metaphysician. The *fact* is that the world would be a hell of a lot better. But my pragmatism does not go so far as to make me believe something is true just because the belief in it makes the world better. The mystic belief is simply nonsensical, and Andricus's hypothesis, though not *logically contradictory,* is empirically ridiculously implausible. Surely there must be *some* saner way of getting people to treat each other better!

ANDRICUS: I also did not want to get sidetracked on moral issues, but I'm afraid that it was mainly my fault for remarking on the ethical ramifications of the concept of my neighbor is myself. But now that we are on the subject of morality, there is something else I wish to say before I come back to the metaphysical and epistemological aspects of the question.

What strikes me as the fundamental difference between the Eastern and Western concepts of morality is this: The Western mind tends to regard one's duty and one's natural inclination as opposing forces. These then are forces in eternal conflict. This conflict is clearly reflected in the Christian theology of God *versus* the devil. Virtue then consists of fighting, resisting, or overcoming temptations. One speaks of the triumph of good over evil. My response is,

"What a way to live!" The very idea of good triumphing over evil structures the situation in such a warlike manner! This is an excellent example of the type of duality that is regarded as so unfortunate by the Easterner. By contrast, the Eastern mind sees no real conflict between egotism and altruism; the apparent conflict arises only from what they call *ignorance*. The entire approach is not to have altruism *triumph* over egotism but to integrate or fuse the two, or rather to realize that they are really one.

I think that the whole situation is beautifully expressed in the Eastern story of the student who asked the master about the true nature of sacrifice. The master replied, "Do not speak to me, my boy, of sacrifice; it is all in the mind! There is much opportunity to do good in the world, and he who does not avail himself of it is robbing himself. Does the sun make a sacrifice by shining forth rays of warmth and light?"

SECOND PHILOSOPHER: Please, Andricus, *can't* we leave the subject of morality and return to the original topic? Your hypothesis was that our minds rotate bodies over various lifetimes, and hence that my neighbor's experiences are either my past or future experiences. Do you seriously regard this as an explanation of what the Eastern mystic means when he says, "Thy neighbor is thyself"?

ANDRICUS: Of course not! No Eastern mystic would accept such a crass, literal-minded interpretation. Only a Westerner like myself would even think of such a thing.

FIRST PHILOSOPHER: Why do you speak so disparagingly of we Westerners? Do you think we are congenitally inferior to the Easterners or something?

ANDRICUS: Of course not. The difference is neither congenital nor a matter of inferiority or superiority. But there *is* a very important difference, as I can assure you from having spent many years in the East. It is that our whole training since early childhood, our whole basic orientation toward life, is so different that we appear almost to have different basic categories of thought. Indeed, some feel that much of the profound wisdom of the East is not even translatable into Western terms. I myself do not go along with this view; I think it is translatable though there are enormous difficulties involved.

At any rate, the hypothesis I suggested was intended only as a first approximation of the notion, "My neighbor is myself." What I now wish to consider is the following variant of this hypothesis: Instead of there being many individual minds in the universe that rotate bodies during successive lifetimes, there is only *one* mind, which inhabits one body at a time—a different one during each physical cycle.

FIRST PHILOSOPHER: This hypothesis strikes me as even crazier than your first!

ANDRICUS: Me, too! It is a rather weird variant of solipsism. Suppose my body should now say, "My mind is the only one in existence." These two physical events would occur over and over again in the various universal cycles. Once and only once when *my* body says it, it will be true; once and only once when *your* body says it, it will be true; and so forth for each body that says it.

SECOND PHILOSOPHER: Since you admit your second hypothesis is even crazier than your first, why did you even bother to formulate it?

ANDRICUS: Mainly in preparation for my third hypothesis, which is as follows: There is only one mind in the universe. This mind very rapidly oscillates through all the living organisms of the universe. it spends, say, a trillionth of a trillionth of a second in your body, then in mine, then in the next fellow's, then in the body of a dog, and so forth. It oscillates so fast that the effect seems continuous, like a single beam of light oscillating all over a television screen.[3]

FIRST PHILOSOPHER: And this, you take it, is an explication of what the Eastern mystic means by the statement, "Your neighbor is yourself"?

ANDRICUS: No, certainly not. Again, this is far too literal, Western, and "science fictitious" to satisfy the Eastern mystic. Indeed, he has —or claims to have—*direct* understanding of the notion, "My neighbor is myself"; no explanation is needed.

FIRST PHILOSOPHER: And do you claim to understand this directly?

ANDRICUS: Yes and no. I might first of all go one step further in the hypothesis: Imagine the one mind oscillating faster and faster. Is it so impossible to pass to the mathematical limit of the situation, which is that the same mind is *simultaneously* in all the different bodies? Indeed, even without passing to this limit, if the oscillation is rapid enough, then for all practical purposes the mind *is* simultaneously in many bodies.

FIRST PHILOSOPHER: Can you honestly say that this idea of your mind being in several bodies *at the same time* does not go counter to your intuition about time?

ANDRICUS: To be perfectly honest, yes! But then I suspect that there is something wrong with our very intuition about time. But we have heard nothing this entire conversation from our friend the epistemologist. Why so silent?

EPISTEMOLOGIST: I have remained silent because my objection to the original statement, "My neighbor is myself," is on such trivially obvious grounds that it seemed almost pointless to voice it.

ANDRICUS: Why not voice it anyhow?

EPISTEMOLOGIST: All right, if you really wish me to I will. How can the statement, "My neighbor is myself," possibly be true? The simple fact is that if a pin is stuck into your body, *you* feel it and *I* don't. It would seem to me that if you and I were identical, then we would either both feel the pain or neither of us feel the pain. How can you say that two things are identical when you affirm something about the one and deny it about the other?

ANDRICUS: Obviously, this is indeed the main objection to the idea and is precisely why the idea is difficult for me to accept.

EPISTEMOLOGIST: Now I don't understand you. Do you accept this Eastern idea or don't you?

ANDRICUS: I told you before, yes and no, by which I mean that in a way I do and in a way I don't. Obviously, the kind of identity the epistemologist used is the Leibnizian notion, which is the notion used by most modern logicians. According to this notion, two things are identical if everything that is true of one of them is also true of the other. In this sense of identity, of course my neighbor is not identical with myself, for the very reason mentioned by the epistemologist.

EPISTEMOLOGIST: Of course I was using the notion of identity in the standard sense. What other sense is there? Any false statement can be made true if one simply changes the meaning of all—or even some—of the words involved. Perhaps you mean by *identical* just what most of us mean by *different*. In *that* nonstandard sense of the word *identical* I will grant you that my neighbor is identical with myself, which now simply means that my neighbor is different from myself.

ANDRICUS: Please now, you hardly think that I am so simple-minded as not to be aware of this completely trivial way of making any statement true. Do you honestly believe that when I affirm the statement, "My neighbor is identical with myself," that by *identical* I mean *different?*

EPISTEMOLOGIST: No, of course I don't believe you are doing anything quite that preposterous! But what *are* you doing? Since you admit that you are not using the notion of identity in the standard sense, you must be using it in some other sense. So instead of tampering with language, why don't you instead use the standard word, or group of words, to describe the notion you have in mind?

ANDRICUS: I assure you that I am not being perverse or trying to be mysterious. The honest fact is that I don't *know* of any other word to convey my meaning.

EPISTEMOLOGIST: And I can assure you that I am not trying to be skeptical for the sake of being skeptical, nor am I trying to be un-understanding. I genuinely believe it possible that you are trying to explicate an extremely important notion, but so far I cannot understand it. Is there *nothing* you can say to make the task any easier for us?

ANDRICUS: There may be something, though I don't know how much it will help. In the first place, though I admitted that my use of the notion of identity is not the Leibnizian notion that logicians use, it does not quite follow that my use is nonstandard; I very much doubt that the Leibnizian notion is the only standard one.

EPISTEMOLOGIST: What other standard notion is there?

ANDRICUS: There is the following: Ask an average adult whether he is the same person he was when he was a child, or whether he is a different person. Some will answer, "Of course I am different; I am taller, fatter, older, wiser, and so forth." Others will answer, "Of course I am the same person. Obviously, I have changed in the meantime, but still I am *really* the same person." My point is that enough people will give the latter answer for it to qualify as standard. Now, this notion of being the *same* person I was when I was a child is obviously not the Leibnizian notion of identity. The adult I and the childhood I do not have all properties in common. In particular, if someone sticks a pin into my present body, the childhood I did not feel it, and if someone sticks a pin in the childhood I, the present I does not feel it. Yet there is, I think, a very real and very important sense in which the childhood I and the adult I are the same. It is *this* notion of identity that comes far closer to the notion of sameness inherent in the statement, "My neighbor is myself."

EPISTEMOLOGIST: I think I understand this other notion of identity (though there are those who would question it). But the two contexts are so very different! In the case of a child becoming an adult, there is an obvious continuity that can easily and naturally give rise to this notion. But comparing you with your neighbor, this continuity is obviously absent, hence how can this other notion of identity apply?

ANDRICUS: Good question! I would answer it by saying that although this other notion of identity would naturally occur to one as a result of continuous transformation, it does not therefore follow that the notion is applicable only in this situation; it may also apply to myself and my neighbor.

FIRST PHILOSOPHER: I think that using pure reason we cannot make much more headway with this problem. At this point, I am afraid that I must ask you an irritatingly practical question. What evidence do you have that your neighbor is yourself?

ANDRICUS: None whatsoever!

FIRST PHILOSOPHER: Then why in heaven's name do you believe it?

ANDRICUS: Why? I don't believe I know why. It just seems right to me.

FIRST PHILOSOPHER: And from the fact that it *seems* right to you, you have the audacity to conclude that it *is* right?

ANDRICUS: Of course not! Of course I know that because something seems right to me it does not follow that it is true. You act as if I started from the premise, "I believe it," and drew as a conclusion, "It is true." But I have done nothing of the sort. The statement, "I believe it," is neither a premise nor a conclusion; it is simply a fact, since I *do* believe it—at least I do much of the time.

FIRST PHILOSOPHER: You mean to say that you believe it some of the time, and some of the time you don't?

ANDRICUS: I'm afraid so!

FIRST PHILOSOPHER: What do you believe at this very moment; do you believe it or not?

ANDRICUS: I'm afraid that at this very moment I feel so silly and on the defensive that I really cannot say whether I believe it now or not.

FIRST PHILOSOPHER: I find it rather ironical that all of us here have been wasting our precious time in what we honestly thought was a genuine objective philosophical discussion, and then it turns out that all you have been saying has led up to a mere *personal* idea, and moreover, one that by your own admission you do not even consistently maintain.

ANDRICUS: In all fairness to myself, I must correct you. I told you at the very beginning of the conversation that I made no *claim* whatsoever; I am merely trying to *understand* the Eastern mystic viewpoint.

SECOND PHILOSOPHER *(to First Philosopher):*   I'm afraid Andricus is right about that, and I must say your attitude can hardly be described as *sympathetic*. But I can also understand your disappointment in expecting a purely objective analysis of the question.

FIRST PHILOSOPHER: Well, I'm sorry if I was overly abrupt, yet I cannot but feel that you, Andricus, instead of consulting us philosophers about this problem should have consulted a psychologist or psychiatrist since your problem is obviously not philosophical but purely psychological.

SECOND PHILOSOPHER: I perfectly agree that the problem is psychological rather than philosophical. Fortunately, I have had some psychiatric training, so I think I can be of some help here.

Look, Andricus, you obviously have some enormously strong *motivation* for wanting to understand and even believe the statement, "Thy neighbor is thyself." You have gone to fantastic lengths in first discussing its ethical ramifications and then bringing in all these weird science fiction fantasies to, as you say, *suggest* its meaning. Then you admit having no *evidence* for its truth and not even a clear knowledge of what it means to be true, and you admit that whatever understanding you *sometimes* have of it is elusive and inconstant. Despite all these difficulties—which you yourself evidently realize—you nevertheless cling to the idea as you would to something very precious. So I must ask you to ask yourself very honestly, What is your *real* motive for embracing this principle?

ANDRICUS: Without having to be as introspective as you suggest, I can certainly think of a very good motive, but I would call this motive philosophical rather than psychological.

SECOND PHILOSOPHER: What motive is that?

ANDRICUS: I was just about to tell you. The statement, "My neighbor is myself," seems to me the only alternative to—of all things—solipsism!

FIRST PHILOSOPHER: Good God, you can't be serious!

MORALIST: Now really, you are going a bit too far!

EPISTEMOLOGIST: How can this statement possibly relate to solipsism?

ANDRICUS: I was just about to tell you. All my life I have never been able to understand how any mind could possibly conceive of anything outside its own experience. How can one mind even *think* of another; what sort of image of it could it possibly have? How could I in all honesty believe in the existence of other minds when I cannot even *conceive* of them?

EPISTEMOLOGIST: What's wrong with the standard argument by analogy? You see other bodies acting sufficiently like your own for you to make a probabilist inference that they have other minds, too.

ANDRICUS: Please, you don't understand! No probabilist argument could help me in the least! In the first place, probabilist arguments have never carried with me the slightest conviction when applied to conclusions that themselves are not empirical.

EPISTEMOLOGIST: I am not sure I understand you.

ANDRICUS: I mean to say that when it comes to predicting directly observable events like the cast of a die, the outcome of spinning a roulette wheel, or the rising of the sun tomorrow, probabilist arguments really carry with me intuitive conviction; they really are causative factors in producing within me psychological *expectation*. But when applied to conclusions that might be called *metaphysical* in nature, as for example, whether external objects really exist, whether minds really exist, whether minds or souls survive bodily death, or whether other minds exist, probabilist arguments just don't carry with me the same type of intuitive conviction. I understand perfectly what is meant by saying that if I throw a die, the probability is 1 in 6 that the number 5 will come up, or that the probability of 17 coming up on a roulette wheel is 1 in 37. But what on earth does it mean to say that the probability that external objects exist is such and such, or that the probability is so and so that other minds exist?

FIRST PHILOSOPHER: But how could we know such things except on a probabilist basis? Everyone who has seriously thought about the matter knows, for example, that solipsism is not logically refutable. From the statement, "My mind is the only one in existence," one certainly cannot derive a logical contradiction. Therefore, I cannot know with logical certainty but only with very high probability that other minds exist. This probability is high enough for my comfort.

ANDRICUS: The probability that other minds exist is high enough for you? Just how high is it, anyhow? Would you care to give a *numerical* estimate of it? Of course not! I still say that probability, as well as logic, is utterly irrelevant to the problem. Most people believe as a matter of course that other minds exist; it would not even occur to them to doubt it, nor to consider, of all things, its probability. Indeed, if an average person should be asked by a philosopher, "How do you *know* that others minds exist?" he will usually look at the philosopher as if he is crazy (and, in a way, he may be right). It is only when one feels the need to justify one's metaphysical beliefs—say, the belief in other minds—that one brings in logic and probability, but these are only afterthoughts or rationalizations and, I maintain, very bad ones at that. The fact is that such beliefs almost always occur *prior* to the arguments found for their justification.

MORALIST: I also believe that the probabilist arguments used to justify the existence of other minds are very poor—indeed, downright immoral. It is simply not very nice to doubt the existence of other minds!

FIRST PHILOSOPHER *(to Moralist):* I'm sorry that I cannot go along with this. Whether other minds exist or not is a fact, and I cannot use a moral argument to establish a question of fact. Besides, to say that it is not nice or that it is immoral to doubt the existence of other minds makes sense only if other minds do in fact exist. If there really were no other minds, why would it be morally wrong to know or to believe this fact? It seems to me that you are putting the cart before the horse. To know whether it is morally right to believe in other minds, it must be first settled whether there *are* other minds, and this, I maintain, can be settled only on the basis of high probability.

ANDRICUS: And I maintain that it cannot. But it is silly for us to argue this point now. If *you* find a probabilist argument necessary for maintaining your belief in other minds, it should hardly be my function to try to deprive you of it. But as I have said before, such an argument carries absolutely no conviction with *me*.

FIRST PHILOSOPHER: In that case, what reasons *do* you have to justify your belief in other minds? Or are you still a solipsist?

ANDRICUS: I still have not made my situation clear to you. I don't require any reasons or justification whatever for the belief in other minds!

FIRST PHILOSOPHER: Then you are not being rational!

ANDRICUS: Call it what you like; we can argue about this another time, since the question of my rationality is so irrelevant to what I am trying to say. As a child, I never had the slightest doubt about the existence of other minds; I took it completely as a matter of course, as most people do. Would you call them irrational for having this belief just because they have never figured out reasons to justify it?

FIRST PHILOSOPHER: Then I am more puzzled than ever. If, as you say, you don't need rational arguments to justify this belief, then what on earth stops you from having it? Why do you have a problem with solipsism at all? Since you don't need any probabilist argument, what stops you from simply accepting the existence of other minds without any inductive evidence?

ANDRICUS: Because of what I told you before. To me, the problem never was, "*Are* there other minds?" but "*Could* there be other minds?" Once I believe that other minds *could* exist, then I would not have the slightest doubt that other minds *do* exist.

FIRST PHILOSOPHER: This is the weirdest argument I have ever heard! You mean to say that you believe that everything that is possible is actual, that everything that *could* exist *does* exist?

ANDRICUS: Of course not! Why do you jump to such a silly generality? I am not saying that everything that can exist does exist. I am just saying that other minds happen to be one of those things whose possible existence would *to me* be enough to ensure their actual existence. In other words, my mind happens to be so constituted, whether rightly or wrongly, rationally or irrationally, that if I can accept the possibility of other minds, then I automatically accept their actuality. I am *not* here drawing any inference or proposing any argument; I am just telling you how I do as a matter of fact think. Normally, I don't do this, but you must recall that I was asked the *psychological* question of what are my *motivations* for my interest in the statement, "Thy neighbor is thyself."

SECOND PHILOSOPHER: So far, so good. I personally could not make the step from the *possibility* of other minds to their actual existence, but if you say that *you* can, who can quarrel with the fact that you do? But I still cannot understand your difficulties in the first place in believing that other minds are even possible. Why should they be impossible?

ANDRICUS: Because, as I told you before, how can I even conceive anything outside of my own experience; hence how can I possibly believe it?

MORALIST: Isn't your attitude just a bit on the egocentric side?

ANDRICUS: Of course it is, and of course I know it! But do you think that knowing it makes matters any easier or less painful? As was said before, how can any *moral* argument clear up an epistemological difficulty? A moral argument might indeed succeed in making one feel guilty for holding certain views, but it cannot possibly succeed in locating the actual source of one's error. Also—since morality has again come up—I think that as an ex-solipsist I should tell you that there is much moral and psychological misunderstanding of the actual state of mind of the solipsist. You act as if the solipsist is an aggressive individual who is trying to aggrandize himself by rejecting others. Has it never occurred to you that a solipsist may be an extremely lonely creature who is desperately trying but does not know how to succeed in *accepting* others?

MORALIST: Oh come on now with your sentimental hogwash! The typical solipsist goes swaggering around with a superior smile saying, "I alone exist, you do not!" Can you seriously expect me to believe that he is anything like the psychological type you describe?

ANDRICUS: The *typical* solipsist? How do *you* know what the typical solipsist is? I doubt very much whether the type you describe is the typical solipsist. I'm afraid that the typical solipsist does not go around publicly announcing his solipsism but bears it shamefully in silence. I wonder whether even the type you do mention is really so vain and proud, underneath it all, or whether he is not covering up a desperate fear and insecurity?

MORALIST: It seems these days that one can excuse any vanity by simply saying that it is only a cover-up for an underlying humility.

SECOND PHILOSOPHER: Leaving aside these moral questions, I would like to return to the basic matter. How does the statement, "Thy neighbor is thyself," help you to believe that the existence of other minds is possible?

ANDRICUS: Because if this statement is true, it means that other minds *do* exist! There can be millions, trillions of them, only they are all identical with my own!

FIRST PHILOSOPHER: Good grief! This is the most utterly insane solution of the solipsism problem that I ever have heard!

MORALIST *(gleefully)*: The man's egotism knows no bounds! *Now* he is saying that *his* mind is the only one in existence, and no other minds exist in the universe; if they do, the only way that they can exist is if they are identical with his! So *his* mind is still the only mind in the universe! If this is not egotism pushed to its utter and fantastic logical extreme, I don't know what is! Perhaps it should no longer be called *egotism* but *superegotism!* I have never before in my entire life heard such a self-aggrandizing doctrine! Furthermore, his brand of solipsism (and after all, it *is* a brand of solipsism) should perhaps be called *supersolipsism.* Compared with standard solipsism, I would say that it is even worse and more vicious!

ANDRICUS *(to Moralist):* Strange as it may seem, I tend to agree with everything you have just said except for your final remark. My viewpoint might indeed be described as pushing egotism to its extreme logical limit. But what is necessarily so bad about that? I have long suspected—as have many others—that altruism is, in the last analysis, nothing more nor less than egotism expanded to its ultimate limit. I also like the terms that you have just coined: *superegotism* and *supersolipsism*. But when you compare supersolipsism with what you call standard solipsism and declare it to be even more vicious, I believe you overlook an important point. When two standard solipsists get together in an argument, each claims the other to be wrong. But I as a supersolipsist can attend a congress of a thousand solipsists, each one shouting, "I am the only mind in existence," and I can happily agree with *all* of them! Each may *think* that all the rest of them are wrong, but I can know that *all* of them are right since they don't actually contradict each other but only think that they do. Each one thinks that he is using the word *I* in a different sense, but in reality they are all using it in the same sense; they mean the same thing by it but don't know it. If I should have the really good fortune of attending a congress of a thousand supersolipsists, it would be even better. Now, when each one said, "I am the only mind in existence," each one would not only *be* right but would know that all the others were also right! I think that rather than call them *supersolipsists*, I would prefer to call them *enlightened solipsists*. Yes, from now on I shall refer to such people as enlightened solipsists. Just think of it! A whole world—a whole universe—peopled with enlightened solipsists! What could be more beautiful!

EPISTEMOLOGIST: I am sorry to interfere with your idyllic fantasies, but I am afraid that there are a few sober questions I must ask you. Your solution of the solipsist problem is certainly nonstandard, to say the least (though I do not think it is wholly original).[4]

The solution is both crazy and ingenious, and I am not wholly insensitive to a certain poetic value. But—with my hard-boiled empiricist training—I cannot let its poetic value seduce me into believing that it really makes any sense. I think that both the craziness and the ingenuity of your viewpoint are more apparent than real. In the last analysis, I think that all you are doing is using words in a nonstandard sense. You say that other minds exist, but they are all identical with yours. To a logician, this is, of course, a straight contradiction since the very word *other* means *not*-identical. But then you get out of it by saying that you are *not* using *identity* in the logician's sense. And when asked in what sense you are using it, you have great difficulty in being precise. Some will say that your inability to define *identity* in your sense indicates that you don't mean anything by it. I am willing to be more charitable and admit that *maybe* you do mean something by it but simply cannot explain what it is.

At any rate, it is clear that you are using language in a highly nonstandard manner. I think the crux of it is this: When you say, "Other minds exist, but they are identical with mine," how do you know that you mean anything more or less than I mean when I say more simply, "Other minds exist"? I think this is really the key question.

ANDRICUS: I would not be the least bit surprised if we meant exactly the same thing.

EPISTEMOLOGIST: In that case, why don't you simply delete the part, "But they are identical with mine," since this is superfluous and only confusing to others?

ANDRICUS: Confusing to others? Unfortunately, it is confusing unless I try to explain. But superfluous? It is not superfluous to me. For without adding this, I simply find it psychologically impossible to believe in other minds! I realize perfectly well how irrational I sound, but which is really more important, that I *talk* rationally or that I actually believe in other minds?

MORALIST: Why this dichotomy? Can't you both be rational *and* believe in other minds? I am perfectly rational, and I believe in other minds. Why can't you be like me?

ANDRICUS: Why *can't* I be like you? I don't know *why* I can't be like you, but the fact is that I simply can't. Who knows, maybe one day I *will* be like you, but for the present I can't. I sincerely envy you—or anybody who is able to integrate rationality with belief in other minds. But so far I have simply not yet found the means to do so.

FIRST PHILOSOPHER: You mean to say that you think that the belief in other minds is irrational?

ANDRICUS: Of course not! What I said was that *I* find it impossible for *me* to both be (or sound) rational and to believe in other minds, which is very different!

SECOND PHILOSOPHER: But what about when you were a child? You told us that in those days you had no difficulty believing in other minds. Did you then have to say, "Other minds exist, but they are all identical with mine"? Did you then have to get enraptured by the notion of enlightened solipsism?

ANDRICUS: Of course not. Those were my days of innocence and true knowledge. As I told you, those were the times when I accepted other minds as a matter of course without any doubts whatsoever— though of course I never verbalized this.

EPISTEMOLOGIST: So what happened to you in the interim?

ANDRICUS: What happened to me? My troubles all started in adolescence when I read the philosophers. Then for the first time bugs were put into my brain: How do you *know* other minds exist? Is it *certain* or only *probable?* What could it *mean* for other minds to exist? How can you possibly think of or believe anything outside your own experience? Having swallowed all this poison, the only way I know how to return to sanity is, unfortunately, by violating language, and talking about such things as enlightened solipsists.

Yet I don't know. Am I really so much worse off than I was before? Just think of it! A world full of enlightened solipsists! What could be more perfect?

Notes

1.   One of my objections to the positivist invitation to reject metaphysical statements since they are cognitively meaningless is that these statements may nevertheless suggest other statements that are meaningful, even in the positivist sense—that may never have occurred to one who had not first seen the others. Similarly, in

mathematics a false proof of a theorem might well suggest a correct one that would never have occurred to one who had not first seen the false one.

2.   George Berkeley, *Complete Works*, Vol. 4, ed. Alexander Campbell Fraser (Oxford: Clarendon Press, 1901), p. 161. Italics are mine.

3.   This is perhaps somewhat reminiscent of the idea of only one physical particle in the entire universe that oscillates all over the universe.

4.   It is not too far from the views of certain mystics, and in a strange sort of way, not too far from Wittgenstein.

13

5000 B.C.

Part I

ANCIENT METAPHYSICIAN: For years I have been trying to find out what keeps the earth up; why does it not fall down? The number of so-called wise men who have claimed to give a satisfactory answer to this problem is appalling! One told me that the earth is resting on another body. When asked upon what this body rests, he described another body. When asked upon what this second body rests, he said, "I have given satisfactory answers to two questions, and that is enough. One can't keep questioning forever!"

This reminds me of an equally exasperating theologian who claimed that there must be a God; otherwise, there could be no explanation for the creation of the universe. But when asked, "How was God created?" he likewise answered, "One can't keep asking questions forever." I replied, "I promise not to keep asking questions *forever;* I think it is unfair of you to stop the enquiry just at the point where you are ahead. So I merely wish to ask but *one* more question; how was God created? If you answer that satisfactorily, I am perfectly willing to end the enquiry there." He replied, "Some things are simply a mystery." I was somewhat softened by the candor of that reply, but as I explained to him, why not simply say that the existence of the universe is a mystery, and let it go at that; why must God be brought in? To put the matter another way, I certainly believe that some things *may* in principle be mysteries, but of what use is a hypothesis for explaining a mystery when the very hypothesis raises another mystery just as baffling as the one it explains?

However, I diverge. Coming back to the question why the earth doesn't fall, I could conceive of the possibility, although I find it rather counterintuitive, that there may be *infinitely* many bodies, each resting on the other, going infinitely far downward with the earth resting on top. Alternatively, perhaps the earth could be resting on a *single* infinite body that extends infinitely downward. Now, this possibility, though rather difficult to believe, does not appear a priori to be completely out of the question. But even if true, I still cannot understand why the earth together with this body wouldn't fall down together as a unit. No, the whole situation is extremely mysterious, and I am honestly very depressed these days at the fact that I simply cannot make any progress in this direction.

FIRST PHILOSOPHER: Perhaps this question is another mystery. That is, it may be totally beyond the powers of any human being ever to find out why the earth stays up.

METAPHYSICIAN: Of course, it *may* be beyond our power, but why should we give up so easily?

SECOND PHILOSOPHER: It may be that in essence your question is unanswerable! The very question itself presupposes a premise, which in fact may be false.

METAPHYSICIAN: What premise is that?

SECOND PHILOSOPHER: The assumption that everything that happens must have a cause or a reason! The earth *does* stay up: That is indeed a fact. But it does not follow that there must be a *reason* for this fact. It may simply be that the earth stays up, and that's all there is to it!

METAPHYSICIAN: Before I answer, let me ask you, Is there any significant difference between your viewpoint and that of the first philosopher, who claimed that the reason why the earth stays up is a mystery?

SECOND PHILOSOPHER: Of course they are different. The first philosopher never doubted, as far as I could tell, that there is a reason why the earth stays up but merely expressed skepticism as to whether the reason can ever be found. I am proposing the more radical hypothesis that there is no reason. There certainly is a difference in these two viewpoints. Indeed, there is a great difference between believing that something exists but not knowing how to find it and believing that the thing doesn't even exist and hence that it is hopeless to even look for it. I believe the latter.

METAPHYSICIAN: I have certainly considered it *possible* that the earth stays up without any reason whatsoever. But I regard such a hypothesis as extremely sterile. If I were to accept it, then I certainly would never find the answer even if there was one and it were in principle discoverable.

FIRST PHILOSOPHER: But you said yourself that you have made absolutely no progress in this direction, so why do you keep paining yourself against such hopeless odds?

METAPHYSICIAN: It is true that I haven't made any overt progress in the sense of having yet come up with any solution. It may be that I have made some latent progress—time will tell. But the point is that if I should adopt either the viewpoint that the answer is an unsolvable mystery or that there is no answer, then I certainly won't find the answer if there is one, whereas if I have faith that there is an answer and that it can be found, then at least I might find it.

ANCIENT POSITIVIST: Has it ever occurred to you that in *principle* you can never find an answer because you are not even asking a question?

METAPHYSICIAN: What on earth are you talking about?

POSITIVIST: I am suggesting that your so-called question is not really a question at all.

METAPHYSICIAN: I still can't understand you!

POSITIVIST: I am saying that the sequence of words, "Why does the earth stay up," though it sounds superficially like a question, is really no question at all; it is merely a meaningless sequence of words.

METAPHYSICIAN: Which words of the sequence are meaningless?

POSITIVIST: I did not say that it is a sequence of meaningless words but that it is a meaningless sequence of words. Of course each word of the sequence is meaningful, but the sequence as a whole is meaningless; it is simply not grammatically formulated.

METAPHYSICIAN: What in the world does *grammar* have to do with why the earth stays up?

POSITIVIST: It is your use of the word *why* that is causing the trouble. This word is of course meaningful in certain contexts but has no meaning in your context.

METAPHYSICIAN: Why not? Or am I again asking a meaningless question?

POSITIVIST: Ignoring this flippancy, I will answer you. When one asks *why* a certain phenomenon occurs, he is simply asking what known general laws account for it. But to ask why the very laws of the cosmos are as they are has no meaning whatsoever. This is really what you are doing in asking why the earth stays up. It is a perfect example of what should be termed a *pseudoquestion,* that is, a sequence of words that sounds like a question but in reality is meaningless.

METAPHYSICIAN: May I ask how you know that the question is meaningless?

POSITIVIST: The answer to this, though elementary in principle, is technically rather involved. After much time and thought, I have finally succeeded in giving an absolutely precise definition of *meaningful;* I have a perfectly exact set of rules called *formation rules for language* with the marvelous property that, given any sequence of words, the rules can decide in a completely mechanical manner whether the sequence is meaningful or not. And it is a simple, demonstrable fact that your pseudoquestion is not meaningful in this perfectly precise sense of *meaningful.*

METAPHYSICIAN: I don't for a moment doubt that you are right! I certainly take your word that according to the rules you have in mind my question is meaningless. But what does this prove? Merely that the question is meaningless according to *your* definition of *meaning*. It does not show that it is meaningless according to *my* notion of *meaning*.

POSITIVIST: What notion is that? Can you precisely define this notion and rigorously prove that your question is meaningful according to a *precise* definition of *meaning*?

METAPHYSICIAN: It seems that you are asking me two somewhat different questions. Do you want me to define *my* notion of *meaning*, or merely to define *some* notion of *meaning* according to which my question is meaningful? The latter is trivial. Of course, given *any* sequence of words, one could easily frame *some* definition of *meaning* according to which the question is meaningful and another according to which it is meaningless. But this strikes me as a completely empty game. The former is of more interest. No, I don't believe that I can define *my* notion of *meaning*. Every definition I have yet heard or yet considered somehow fails to hit the mark; it almost always leaves out something that I would call *meaningful*.

POSITIVIST: Ah, then you admit that you don't have a precise notion of meaning!

METAPHYSICIAN: It is not clear to me that the inability to define a notion necessarily indicates the lack of precision of that notion. A dog cannot define a bone, but he knows what to do with it, and I would say his notion of a bone is as clear and precise as yours or mine.

No; I certainly think that one should carefully distinguish between the following three things: (1) meaning something by a word, or group of words; (2) knowing what one means; and (3) being able to explain what one means.

POSITIVIST: Well, if you cannot explain to me your notion of meaning, perhaps I can form some idea by considering some examples. Suppose someone asked you, "Why is red?" Would you label this as meaningless or meaningful?

METAPHYSICIAN: I certainly can perceive absolutely no meaning to that question whatsoever. No one has ever asked me such a question (except perhaps in jest). If someone seriously asked it, I would surely be quite puzzled. As I said, *I* can see no meaning in it; it is meaningless to *me*. But I would hate to label it as downright meaningless. I don't consider it very nice to stigmatize another's words as meaningless.

POSITIVIST: Oh come now, you are just being excessively polite! Why should the truth be hidden just to spare another's feelings? You know damn well that, "Why is red?" is completely meaningless!

METAPHYSICIAN: I know that it is meaningless to me, and I am quite sure it is meaningless to almost everyone. But from this, I cannot conclude that it is meaningless to *him*.

POSITIVIST: I am not talking about the *subjective* notion of being meaningful to a given person; I am speaking about *meaning* in a purely objective sense.

METAPHYSICIAN: The only sense I can significantly attach to *objectively meaningful* is *subjectively meaningful to a large number of persons*. If this is all you mean by *objectively meaningful,* then of course the question, "Why is red?" is objectively meaningless in this sense. But I doubt that is what you do mean since this definition would fail to exclude my question, "Why does the earth stay up?" No one to whom I ever have previously asked this question has failed to understand what it *means;* they have merely not known the answer. Indeed, you are the first person I have ever met who rejects the very question itself as meaningless. That you do this strikes me, I must confess, as utterly astonishing!

POSITIVIST: The question has the same fault as so many other "questions" asked by metaphysicians. For example, consider what is perhaps the most ancient, and about the most senseless, metaphysical question of all: "Why is it that there is something instead of nothing?" Would you regard that as a meaningful question?

METAPHYSICIAN: Of course I would! How could one possibly fail to understand this question?

POSITIVIST: I should have guessed you would call this question meaningful; it is so analogous to your so-called question. Let me put it this way: Do you agree that for a question to be meaningful there must in principle exist at least a possibility of an answer?

METAPHYSICIAN: Of course.

POSITIVIST: And do you further agree that there must in principle exist some possible experience that the questioner could have that would constitute an answer?

METAPHYSICIAN: Yes.

POSITIVIST: Then let us stop kidding around. I ask you point-blank: What conceivable experience could you envision that would constitute an answer?

METAPHYSICIAN: I have no idea what such an experience could be! If I knew that, I might be well on the road to finding the answer.

POSITIVIST: So you mean to say that you can regard a question as meaningful even though you have no conception of what kind of an experience would constitute an answer?

METAPHYSICIAN: Of course I would say that! I have many times been puzzled by questions and had no idea what the answer could even be like until I found it. Indeed, I have sometimes even had a wrong idea about what the answer could be like, and when I found the real answer, I realized that I could never have anticipated what it would be like in a million years.

POSITIVIST: If you find an answer, will you know it?

METAPHYSICIAN: Obviously. What a silly question!

POSITIVIST: But how will you recognize the answer when you have found it?

METAPHYSICIAN: I don't know *how* I will recognize it; I will just recognize it, and that's all there is to it!

POSITIVIST: Will you be capable of communicating your answer to others?

METAPHYSICIAN: I am no mystic. If I could not communicate my answer to others, I would not regard the answer as altogether satisfactory.

POSITIVIST: I still would like to know *how* you will recognize an answer when you find one.

METAPHYSICIAN: You sound like an inquisitor! Let me ask you honestly, Why are you so intent on convincing me that my question is meaningless?

POSITIVIST: Please don't get so upset! My motives are not as harsh as you might suspect. I am not trying to show that you are stupid or to belittle you in any way. I am indeed trying to influence you to give up this question, but for your own good!

METAPHYSICIAN: Now what kind of nonsense is this!

POSITIVIST: It's not such nonsense. I cannot help but be concerned at the great number of talented minds like yours who have fallen into purely linguistic traps and are wasting time torturing themselves on speculations that in principle can never lead anywhere. I think that if you would have the patience to listen to my admittedly formalistic and rather dull theory of meaning, then you would fully realize that your question is meaningless and would soon give up asking it.

METAPHYSICIAN: The former perhaps, but certainly not the latter. Perhaps your motives are as good as you say, but if you are going to take this approach, then even from a purely psychological viewpoint, I don't think it is sound. All right, suppose that by superior logic you could drive me into a corner and compel me to admit—totally against my own intuition—that my question is meaningless. Do you think for one moment that this would in any way dispel my *feeling* for the meaning of the question? Do you really think that I would be any the less puzzled by why the earth stays up or would in any way cease to try to find out?

ANCIENT PSYCHOLOGIST: I definitely agree with the positivist that your question is pathological, but I disagree with his method of treatment. It is obvious to me that you are suffering from a purely concrete problem that you do not wish to face, so you have trans-ferred all your compulsive anxieties to a purely abstract level on which you feel more safe. But you will never be able to get rid of the question by remaining on the level of philosophical abstractions. You can succeed only by solving the concrete problem that gave rise to it, in which case the philosophical question will disappear by itself. If only you had been brought up right, you would never ask such questions to begin with.

EASTERN MYSTIC: It is as I have been saying for years! If only the metaphysician would follow my exercises in breathing and meditation, then after a few months the question would disappear as if by magic.

PSYCHOLOGIST: I am afraid this approach is not very realistic! The metaphysician is obviously suffering from a concrete problem that was incurred in his early childhood. No amount of breathing or meditating is going to unearth this problem.

MYSTIC: I would say that his problem was incurred long, *long* before his childhood, but let that pass for the present. Even if his problem does have the genesis that the psychologist claims, it does not follow that the only or even best way to cure it is by remembering it. I have simply observed, in a purely hard-boiled empirical sense, that my exercises do relieve this type of problem without giving the kind of insight so valued by the psychologist. From my point of view, his true problem far transcends any events of his childhood. His real problem consists of his existential anxiety in not knowing who he really is and not knowing his true relationship to the cosmos. For this, no mere analysis of the events of his present life cycle will avail.

POSITIVIST: I think both your approaches are unnecessarily and highly indirect. It may indeed be true that the *genesis* of his problem is what the psychologist or what the mystic claims. But this is only the genesis. The problem itself is on a purely linguistic level and is perfectly capable of being treated on this level. After all, the metaphysician is an extremely intelligent human being and is capable of reason. He, like so many of us, has been enslaved by linguistic habits that lead to the asking of pseudoquestions. But this can be explained to him on a completely conscious and rational level.

PSYCHOLOGIST: I say you are wrong! No rational, linguistic analysis will help cure his malady. His problem is psychosexual, not linguistic.

MYSTIC: I say you are both wrong; his real problem is existential.

POSITIVIST: No, no; his real problem is linguistic!

Part II

At this point, the metaphysician quietly left the company, who were far too engrossed in diagnosing his condition even to notice his absence. After wandering about for awhile, the bitter irony of the whole situation really came upon him. The whole company unanimously considered that the solution to his problem was to cease asking the question rather than to successfully find an answer; they disagreed only on what technique could be used to help him cease his enquiry.

A few weeks after this episode, the metaphysician discovered the secret of time travel! He came to the twentieth century, where I met him a few months after his arrival. He had already mastered English perfectly. We struck up a close friendship almost immediately, and he spent his remaining few months of the twentieth century as a guest at our house in Tannersville. He adored my dogs, who barked joyously on his arrival. He loved romping with them in the mornings; the afternoons and evenings he spent mostly in our library. He mastered most of the extant philosophy in a phenomenally short period.

One day, as we were sitting in the library, I asked him how long it took him to find out the answer to his main question, "Why does the earth stay up?" He replied, "Almost immediately on arrival. Every schoolboy knows today that the word *up* has no absolute meaning." I then asked him, "Do you today regard the positivist as right or wrong when he declared your question meaningless?" He smiled and replied, "In a way he was right, but for the wrong reasons! He totally misled me by saying that the word *why* was the cause of the trouble. It was obviously the word *up* that was the true cause (though nobody in my time could have suspected it). Since the word *up* has no absolute meaning, then of course the question, 'Why does the earth stay up?' has no absolute meaning. But yet I now know the answer! The most remarkable thing that I have learned from this whole experience is something that I never would have dreamed or suspected, namely, that it is not always necessary for a question to be meaningful to obtain an answer. I now obviously know *why* the earth doesn't fall down; there simply *is* no such thing as down. But I could never have known the meaninglessness of this question without first having found the answer! So if I had listened to the positivist, I might have assented to the fact that the question is meaningless, but I never could have really believed it and never could have known *why* it is meaningless. Besides, had I listened to him, I never would have traveled to the future with the hopes of finding an answer."

The one topic my friend was secretive about was his method of time travel. When I expressed utter amazement that this could have been discovered in 5000 b.c., he smiled and said, "Your twentieth-century science fiction is totally off the path concerning the correct method. It does not require technology, elaborate machinery, or sources of great energy. The true method of propelling oneself into the future is so ridiculously simple, so obvious, so under our very noses, that virtually no one can perceive it." He then went on to say that he did not withhold the secret to be mysterious but felt certain that if the method were generally known, man would make a vast exodus to the future and too few people would remain to support the future, hence all would perish.

In his last few days with me, his philosophic interests centered mainly around the twentieth-century positivist and analytic schools. His bitterness knew no bounds. For example, upon seeing the title, "The Elimination of Metaphysics," he exclaimed in horror, "Eliminate metaphysics! Who in his right mind would want to eliminate such a beautiful subject!" To a large extent, I share his feelings. But I still felt duty-bound (partly out of loyalty to friendships I have had with empiricist philosophers) to offer some defense. I pointed out to him that a vast amount of metaphysical trash has been generated in the past, some of it downright fraudulent, and that we shouldn't be too hard on those of intellectual integrity who—though perhaps somewhat misguided—have made a sincere effort to combat this nonsensical activity. He replied, "I am fully aware of this, but they are throwing out the baby with the bathwater. Of course their program, if successful, would eliminate much phony metaphysics, but it would also eliminate some of the most beautiful, sincere, and sublime metaphysics produced by the human race." He also felt that many of the positivists were in a way just downright stupid. He asked, "Can they for one moment have any doubt that any of the earlier competent metaphysicians would have totally agreed with them that their metaphysical questions *were* metaphysical and had no *cognitive* meaning whatsoever? But obviously, to a metaphysician cognitive meaning is but a tiny part of meaning in general, so why should the lack of cognitive meaning of their enquiries encourage them to give them up?"

He also made another point that struck me quite forcibly. He sensed, particularly of the early positivists, a certain *heartlessness* to their approach. As he eloquently expressed it, "They remind me of hardhearted parents whose child is crying and complaining of some sort of pain or disturbance but whose knowledge of language is yet too limited to express exactly what or where the trouble lies, and the parents then respond, 'Unless you can formulate your trouble more precisely, don't bother me with your complaints!' "

I tried to point out to the metaphysician that, particularly in more recent years, the analytic tradition had something to contribute that was of real value even to the metaphysicians themselves, namely, that some light might be thrown on certain philosophical disputations as to whether they are real or only verbal. To use an analogy, imagine two societies living side by side in which one of them, for some strange reason, had got the words *circle* and *ellipse* interchanged. Imagine now two children, one from each society, standing before a geometrical figure and bitterly arguing, "It is a circle"; "No, it is an ellipse"; "No, it is a circle"; "No, it is an ellipse"; and so forth. Clearly, their difference is not real but semantical. To go one step further, imagine two children of whom we do not know whether they belong to the same or to different societies looking at a figure that is *very* slightly elliptical; almost a perfect circle, but so faintly elliptical that about half the people would be sensitive enough to perceive it as an ellipse, and the other half would see it as a perfect circle. Now suppose the two children were having the same argument. We could not possibly tell (without further questions) whether they *saw* it differently or only disagreed verbally. (Similarly, if they agreed verbally, we could not know whether their agreement was *real* or merely verbal.) It is here that something in the spirit of analytic philosophy could be helpful. We could, for example, ask the one who claimed it circular, "Is it *very* circular or only slightly circular?" The metaphysician saw the point.

It was sad when the day of parting came. He could not go back to his own time: Backward time travel, he assured me, was totally impossible. But he longed to investigate further into the future. Much as I knew I would miss him, I did not press him to stay. We said our parting words, and warmly shook hands. He then sat in a chair opposite me, smiled, waved goodbye, and quite suddenly vanished.

Afterthoughts

Some General Comments

Several people have asked me where I stand in all these matters. For example, in my piece "Simplicus and the Tree," do I identify myself with the realistic mystic? Well, I certainly find several aspects of this position of interest, but it is hardly my own. It seems to me that he is essentially an Aristotelian who identifies soul and pattern, which I assuredly do *not* do! To me, pattern is something purely abstract, whereas soul (or mind or psyche) is as concrete as anything can be. I believe that one of the most tragic philosophical errors of our time is the identification of the abstract with the concrete. For example, a well-known computer scientist recently said, "What's the difference between the universe and the set of differential equations that describes it?" How anyone can identify something as concrete as a universe with anything as abstract as a set of equations is totally beyond my comprehension. No, I am surely *not* the realistic mystic. If anything, I would tend to identify with the first Zen master. I heartily agree that statements such as, "I am enjoying this tree," are perfectly comprehensible without any analysis. In a strange sort of way, I also identify with Simplicus.

When I once read "An Epistemological Nightmare," to one well-known logician, I was utterly amazed that he could not see why it was funny. He regarded the experimental epistemologist as perfectly sensible! Really now, to have more confidence in a machine's report of the nature of one's experience than in the experience itself. How crazy can one get? Besides, even from a purely logical point of view, one's knowledge of the machine's report is obtained only through other experiences (seeing where the needles of the dial point, etc.), and so why should *those* experiences be held more trustworthy than the experiences being tested? I was thinking of adding another scene to this chapter in which there was a second epistemologist present using a brain-reading machine on the first epistemologist at the same time the first one was using a machine on Frank. Then when the first one says to Frank, "Wrong, the book does *not* seem red to you," the second one asks the first, "How do you know he is wrong?"

When the first answers, "The dials of my machine are reading 17–06–42–87," the second asks, "How do you know the dials are reading those numbers?"

The first replies, "It seems that way to me."

The second epistemologist then says, "It *doesn't* seem that way to you!"

Do I make my point?

What Can One Expect from Philosophy?

Aside from my obvious dislike of moralists, the one bias I have clearly shown in this book is my negative attitude toward logical positivism, but even here I have some reservations. I recently read Brand Blanshard's book *Reason and Analysis* in which he attacked positivism and much of positivist-oriented analytic philosophy.[1] Needless to say, I was delighted with his views and with his skillful use of positivistic techniques against positivism itself. But for some amazing reason, the overall effect of reading it has been to make me more sympathetic to positivism than I was before. Let me explain.

I believe that much of the antagonism toward positivism has resulted, so to speak, from the tone of voice or style of its writings rather than their objective content. For example, the very title, "The Elimination of Metaphysics," would immediately put anyone with metaphysical interests into an antagonistic frame of mind. It is a pity that Carnap did not choose some alternative title, such as "On the Necessary Limitations of Metaphysics." Such a title would surely antagonize no one; indeed, it would attract even the metaphysicians themselves. I think the fact is that positivists, particularly the early ones, have been quite hostile to metaphysics (which is quite understandable in view of some of the loose and sloppy work done by metaphysicians) and that their hostility clearly showed through their writings and aroused counterhostility on the part of many readers. This counterhostility may well have prevented, or at least delayed, recognition of what I feel are the useful and positive aspects of positivism. This now brings me to my central point.

Suppose I have a world view that is internally perfectly consistent, that is, logically consistent, consistent with all the experiences I have ever had, and consistent with all my feelings and intuitions. For the moment, let us make the further assumption (totally unrealistic as it almost certainly is) that the view is consistent with any experience I ever will have in the future. Let us call such a view a *perfect world view*. Now suppose that you also have a perfect world view but that yours is logically incompatible with mine. It seems to me that the valuable contribution of the positivists (and, for that matter, the pragmatists) is the realization of the question, "How *in principle* could you or I ever show each other to be wrong?" In other words, can we really hope to get anything more from philosophy than consistency? But suppose that you and I are both Platonists and that we are not at all satisfied that our views are merely consistent; we both believe in a real world, and we each affirm our views to be true of this real world. These Platonic principles, let us assume, are themselves perfectly consistent with the rest of our perfect world views, and so we both adopt them. The positivists might tell us that we are both wrong in asserting that each other's views are false since there exists no way of verifying them (from the outside). But you and I both add as further axioms to our systems, "The positivists are wrong," and let us say our systems are still consistent. Now what can the poor positivist do? In principle, he cannot convince us that our rejection of positivism is wrong. I might also add that although it may be true that in principle we cannot convince each other, it may be *consistent* for us to claim that we can. So we add as further axioms to our systems, "There is some principle that (if only we could find it!) can show that the other one is wrong," and we still have consistent systems. I think this is equivalent to our each denying that the other's world view *is* perfect. It could well be that our world views are in fact perfect, yet it might be consistent for each of us to deny that the other's world view is perfect. (Indeed, it might even be consistent to deny that one's *own* world view is perfect!) Actually, if I believed your world view to be perfect (though false), I think I am now sufficiently influenced by the positivists to realize that my arguing with you could be of no avail. Thus, I think that our very process of arguing with each other indicates our lack of belief in the perfection of each other's world views; we hope either to show the other view to be inconsistent or to produce some new experience in the other person that will change his mind or call forth to full consciousness some latent intuition. This, I think, is what metaphysicians of the past have been up to. As Carnap has rightly pointed out, metaphysicians are not content just to present their systems (unlike artists and poets, who only present their works of art), but they try to *refute* the metaphysical systems of others. I have just proposed what I believe this refutation to really be.

Suppose now that you and I believe that each other's world views are perfect (but false). Although it is senseless for us to argue with each other (even on the friendliest possible basis!), does it make no sense for us to philosophize together at all? No, I believe there is something very valuable left to be done. Let me, for the moment, describe the situation from my viewpoint. Since your world view is consistent, then (making an analogy to mathematical logic) there is *some* interpretation of all your terms under which everything you say is true. Let us assume that our terminology is the same, that is, we use the same words but not necessarily with the same meanings. Indeed, our meanings must be different since some of your statements are refutable in my system. But at any rate, since your system is consistent, then everything you say is true under *some* interpretation of our language. So instead of my saying, "You are wrong," it would make more sense for me to say, "You are wrong according to *my* meanings of our words." The important point to realize (and I don't know if I can convey to the reader the startling impact of this realization) is that according to a mere reinterpretation of the language, *everything you say is true about the real world!* Even if you should deny the existence of a real world and the notions of truth and meaning, *there is some interpretation of all this* that is true about the real world and that may be of extreme interest and value for me to know. The point, then, is, in mathematical language, to construct a model of your language within mine. Put less precisely, though more expressively, the point is for me to be able to see the world through your eyes. After having gone through such an experience, it is more than likely that my own world view might become considerably enlarged. After all, even in a perfect world view, one has not necessarily decided the truth of every statement; there may be many alternative ways of extending it to produce a more comprehensive perfect world view. The very process of modeling another's consistent world view within one's own might be just the thing to decide hitherto undecidable propositions.

To the reader with some knowledge of mathematical logic, I acknowledge that I of course realize that my fanciful analogies have their weak points. For example, I have treated a world view as if it were a formalized first order language, which of course it isn't (at least I hope it isn't! I would feel rather sorry for one whose world view is!). Also, the notion of a *perfect* world view is of course highly idealized; I doubt that anyone even has a world view consistent with all the experiences he has already had! But I believe that all I have said about perfect world views should apply a fortiori to those that are not perfect.

The technique of philosophizing that I am suggesting might be put in the form of a maxim: "Instead of trying to prove your opponent wrong, try to find out in what sense he may be right." This is a sort of tolerance principle, not too unrelated to that of Carnap.[2] To repeat my main point, much may be gained from constructing possible models of other world views within one's own. I believe that this is in the spirit of much of modern analysis. But I would like to see this applied more to some of the great metaphysical systems of the past.

Notes

1. Brand Blanshard, *Reason and Analysis*, The Paul Carus Foundation Lecture XII (La Salle: Open Court Publishing Co., 1964).

2. Indeed, it can be thought of as a semantic counterpart of Carnap's principle of tolerance. His principle says that a language should be regarded as acceptable if it is consistent—or, equivalently, if it has a model. My principle is to try to find such a model—or rather an interesting model of the language.